——— TH[E]

RALPH D. WINTER

——— STORY ———

HOW ONE MAN DARED TO

SHAKE UP WORLD MISSIONS

HAROLD FICKETT

WILLIAM CAREY
LIBRARY

Published by William Carey Library
1605 E. Elizabeth Street
Pasadena, CA 91104 |www.missionbooks.org

Kelley K. Wolfe, editor
Brad Koenig, copyeditor
Alyssa E. Force, graphic design

Cover photo and interior photos courtesy of USCWM photo archive

William Carey Library is a ministry of the
U.S. Center for World Mission
Pasadena, CA | www.uscwm.org

Printed in the United States of America

17 16 15 14 13   5 4 3 2 1 BP4000

Library of Congress Cataloging-in-Publication Data

Fickett, Harold.
 The Ralph D. Winter story : how one man dared to shake up world missions /
  Harold Fickett. p. cm.
 ISBN 978-0-87808-496-8
 1. Winter, Ralph D. 2. Missiologists--United States--Biography. 3. Missions--
Theory--History--20th century. 4. Roberta Winter Institute I. Title.
 BV2072.2.W56F53 2012
 266.0092--dc22
 [B]

2012015147

CONTENTS

To Bob and Chris

FOREWORD

Novelist Jerome Weidman met Albert Einstein one time back in the 1950s. A short time later he published a brief essay, "The Night I Met Einstein." That essay has become a classic and one of the most requested articles ever published in the long history of *Readers' Digest*.

Shortly after joining the Trinity faculty in the mid-1960s, I met Ralph Winter for the first time. He was already something of a legend for making the required course in world missions one of Fuller's most exciting offerings. Naturally, I inquired as to how he did it. Winter responded in the following vein:

> After coming here I soon found out that most graduate-level students think that the Christian mission is important but simple, and that mission courses are "Mickey Mouse." So my first objective is to demonstrate that, whether viewed as theology or science, there is very little that one can learn that is not applicable to the worldwide mission of the church. In no time at all students are reading materials they have never seen, pondering problems they have never considered, and finding solutions they have never contemplated. From that point it's a "piece of cake."

For me, Dr. Winter's answer proved to be a window on his entire ministry. It was to be my good fortune to meet with him numerous times and in various venues for over half a century. On almost every occasion I was blessed with insights and faced with challenges reminiscent of "the day I met Winter." Numerous others have had similar experiences. And, now, still many more will be instructed and challenged by reading and studying *The Ralph D. Winter Story*. This book will become a classic—required reading for anyone interested in the mission of the church. Why? Because a complete knowledge of modern missions is now—and will be in the future—unattainable apart from an understanding of the life, thoughts, and works of this remarkable man.

David J. Hesselgrave
Lindenhurst, Illinois

ACKNOWLEDGMENTS

This work began as a collaborative project with Ralph D. Winter, as we intended to write a book together about his later thinking, especially in regard to the Roberta Winter Institute and its initiatives. For this reason I had the privilege of coming to know Ralph in the last years of his life. His candor, immense energy, ironic humor, lack of guile, capacity for friendship, and most of all, the intimacy he knew with Christ, made our too-brief working sessions together a pleasure and a gift. I enjoyed being in his company and have continued to do so mentally (and I think, spiritually, in the communion of the saints) during the writing. He was highly idiosyncratic, which could drive others crazy, but for me that twinkle that came into his eye when he encountered life's absurdity and made a quick joke that you'd miss if you weren't on your toes more than compensated for his at-times abrupt manner. Unlike almost every other Christian leader with whom I've worked—and I've known my share—he didn't pretend to be interested in you; he actually was interested, because God's drama engaged him far more than his own part in it. So my thanks first to Ralph—for God is the God of the living, eternally.

Ralph's wife, Barb, accompanied me on this journey every step of the way and proved nearly as indefatigable and tenacious in her care for this book as an editor as she was for Ralph as his help-mate. She is a brilliant woman in her own right, and one of the best content editors with whom I've ever worked.

Thanks to Ralph and Roberta's daughters—Beth, Becky, Linda, and Tricia—for reading the manuscript carefully and correcting a few false impressions and errors of fact. I also appreciate their understanding that this is my view of their father and of how some of the situations in which he found himself played themselves out, when their own perspectives differ.

Beth Snodderly, president of William Carey International University, who has devoted so much of her thinking and life to Dr. Winter, steered me in the right direction toward countless resources and was, stage by stage, an invaluable commentator on the manuscript as it developed, as well as being enormously hospitable when I visited the campus in Pasadena.

Ralph's longtime associate Bruce Graham was also of particular help with background interviews, which filled in my understanding of how the U.S. Center for World Mission developed and provided perspective on how Ralph approached certain problems.

Ralph's successor as general director of the Frontier Mission Fellowship, Dave Datema, provided an overview of where the FMF has been and will be going in the future.

Brian Lowther, the executive director of the Roberta Winter Institute, kept me informed on developments with this key initiative and invited me to planning sessions where I gained a fuller appreciation of exciting future developments.

No one who takes even the briefest glance at the references will miss the central importance of Greg Parsons' dissertation to uncovering so many of the source documents that were especially helpful. He did the hard, scholarly work, which I am making use of for a popular audience. It takes a particular humility for the scholar who really knows the subject to let a storyteller like me mine his hard-won research. The substance of Greg's dissertation particularly influenced my understanding of the Winters' life in Guatemala and Ralph's time at Fuller.

I also had considerable help from John Spears, who helped me complete my research and put together early drafts of a few chapters. I have been in John's shoes many times, and I know that "life in the acknowledgments section" never adequately describes the role such an assistant plays in a manuscript's construction. Thank you, John.

I want to thank my family—my wife, Karen; and my children, Hal, Will, and Eve—without whom I'd be lost.

Finally, a word to the dedicatees, Bob and Chris. These outstanding men set me back on my feet during a difficult job transition. Indeed, this book was written, semimiraculously, in the midst of a long crisis that I came through because of their counsel and friendship. They were and are the love of Christ to me.

A GENIUS FOR GOD

In the summer of 1974, Christian leaders gathered in Switzerland for the evangelical Protestant equivalent of Vatican II. Twenty-seven hundred representatives from a hundred and fifty nations at the Lausanne Congress on World Evangelization considered whether the whole world might be evangelized by the year 2000. Billy Graham called the congress together. England's leading evangelical, John Stott, spoke, as did East Africa's Bishop Festo Kivengere, South America's Rene Padilla, and Susumu Uda of Tokyo. Popular apologist Francis Schaeffer came down from his study center, L'Abri, in nearby Huémoz, to address the gathering. The schedule was replete with such luminaries. None made the lasting impact, though, of an idiosyncratic professor from California's Fuller Seminary named Dr. Ralph D. Winter. Winter's speech accomplished nothing less than fixing Lausanne's attention on more than 2 billion "unreached peoples," reigniting cross-cultural evangelism, while restoring to many of the delegates and their organizations a reason for being.

Winter's epoch-making speech began in the most unpromising way. He apologized, awkwardly, that his remarks might end in confusion. The texts of the plenary addresses, like Winter's, had been circulated beforehand, with several experts scheduled to speak in response. For scheduling reasons, those responding to Winter's paper actually spoke before Winter himself. His points were critiqued from the podium before he made them. In these circumstances Dr. Winter chose to respond briefly to his critics with cobbled-together remarks and then proceeded to the substance.

Ralph Winter was not quite fifty years old. In the Day-Glo 1970s, when even Billy Graham's hair trailed over his collar, Dr. Winter looked like a throwback to the black-and-white 1950s. He wore a plain, dark suit and bow tie. His was of average height, slim, mostly bald, and he wore half glasses for reading his notes. He initially spoke in an urgent deadpan, like the announcer at the beginning of early sci-fi pictures. He came across as the Caltech-trained engineer he had once been, a Mr. Wizard or "Bill Nye the Science Guy," illustrating his speech with complicated charts. Here was a man born to wear a pocket protector.

Winter was far more than an entertaining popularizer, though. He belonged in that class of intrepid thinkers, populated by Buckminster Fuller, his old Caltech professor Linus Pauling, and Segway inventor Dean Kamen, who are ready to tackle any problem that attracts their attention. His peculiar genius lay in turning a first-class scientific mind to the problems of world evangelization. He referred to himself as a "social engineer."

Despite its unpromising beginning—and the charts—Winter's speech would be interrupted twice by applause before its passionate conclusion brought down the house.

The second time applause broke out, Dr. Winter remarked, off the cuff, "Now don't clap too soon because this is a really nitty gritty question." The audience laughed, as did Ralph. He was not above having a laugh in the midst of what would be remembered as the most important speech of his life. He had a fine appreciation of life's absurdities, and the ridiculous put a twinkle in his eye.

In its written version, his speech came to be called, "The New Macedonia: A Revolutionary New Era in Mission Begins." In the spoken version, after acknowledging his respondents' helpful correctives, Ralph Winter summed up the position of the Christian movement vis-à-vis the rest of the world and clarified, as no one else, the nature of the task before it. He freed the delegates from

false assumptions that would have made the task impossible.
He spoke to their deepest suspicions and misgivings. He showed
how the way forward had been anticipated in the first years of
the church's existence, when the Holy Spirit revealed Christianity
to be a faith at home in any culture. The faith's strength lay in its
capacity to hop from one culture to another across the centuries, as
old centers lapsed into passivity and frontiers became new capitals.

At that time there were 2.7 billion people in the world who
were not Christians—1 million for each delegate to the Lausanne
Congress. Of these, 83 percent were Muslim, Hindu, Buddhist, or
secular Chinese. These statistics would seem to mandate that by far
the greater part of efforts in cross-cultural evangelism should have
been directed toward these groups. In fact, 95 percent of evangelistic efforts were directed at the 17 percent of non-Christians
who were neither Muslim, nor Hindu, nor Buddhist, nor Chinese.
An enormous task had yet to be done.

Winter's assertion contradicted what most accepted or feared
true. It was the settled wisdom of the missions community that
Christianity never truly takes hold in a country until that nation
has a thriving church run by nationals. There must be a Korean
church for the Koreans; a Nigerian church for the Nigerians. The
remarkable success of both these national churches proved this
true, whereas the failure of the Japanese church to become something more than a Western import kept it small and without much
influence. At the time of the Lausanne Congress almost all of the
world's *nations* had Christian churches—of one denominational
stripe or another. Even an overwhelming and at-times ruthless
Muslim nation like Afghanistan had a fledgling church—one
Ralph Winter had done much to encourage by helping to send
J. Christy Wilson and dozens of others there. (Ralph's interest in
Afghanistan grew as a result of his family hosting Ali Askar from
Afghanistan for a year when Ralph was in high school.) It ap-
peared that the era of cross-cultural evangelism—the era of India's
William Carey and China's Hudson Taylor—had come to an end.

Further, most mission agencies were all too conscious of how missionaries had at times abetted the predations of colonialism and wanted to get out of the business of carrying on "the white man's burden," as Rudyard Kipling put it. Twenty years before, when Ralph Winter and his wife had first gone to Guatemala as missionaries, they had been called "fraternal workers," as were all Presbyterian missionaries, implying they were only in the country to assist the indigenous church, not run it. Western Christian leaders feared that "missions work" had too often been confused with meddling in other people's national churches.

In his written paper—and in the body of his work that many of the delegates already knew—Winter established that every nation had its national church only if nationality were defined in the often-arbitrary way of geographic borders. Within China, for example, many "nations" existed, in the sense of distinct peoples, each with its own language and culture. These nations or people groups often lived in close proximity to one another and yet were as different as American white Anglo-Saxon Protestants are from Bengalis.

Winter's understanding of "people groups" came from the groundbreaking work of his colleagues at Fuller Theological Seminary, Donald McGavran and Alan Tippett. The three Fuller professors recognized that the true dimensions of the task of evangelization would never be recognized unless the Christian world began to think in terms of people groups rather than geographical nations. Each people group should have its own independently thriving church in order to be considered adequately evangelized.

If one looked at the world in terms of people groups rather than modern nations, Winter argued, some 2.3 billion people and their succeeding generations would remain unevangelized if the extremely difficult task of cross-cultural evangelism did not become the church's highest priority.

Winter devoted much of his written paper to distinguishing three types of evangelism. Most commonly, people are called upon to present Christ's message and embody his love to their neighbors—people with whom they share a common language, culture, and similar social status.

Others traverse borders of language, culture, and social position but remain within the same civilization, as when an American ministers in Europe or parts of the world that have been Westernized.

The most difficult evangelism takes the missionary out of his own culture. It often involves learning a language that has no common foundation with a missionary's mother tongue—or even a written basis or grammar. (Winter crossed these frontiers earlier in his career when he ministered to the Mam people in Guatemala.) Truly cross-cultural evangelism places a missionary in societies whose language, ethnicity, and worldview are profoundly distinct from the missionary's home culture.

Evangelism that takes a missionary from one civilization into another may be so difficult that one of Winter's respondents raised the possibility that it should not be attempted at all. Winter understood it was best for someone from within a community to evangelize a people whenever possible. He insisted, though, that obedience to Christ demands crossing every type of frontier and boundary when there are no other options.

One might think this to be an unexceptionable point for the gathering in Lausanne. Many resisted Winter's analysis, however, because they truly believed there was no longer any need for Westerners to evangelize "the heathen."

The missions community had jumped to this conclusion because it aligned its stance with the American Civil Rights Movement. Public institutions, and certainly the church, should be "integrated" whenever possible, expressing the unity we have in Christ. Every nation should have but one church, and the proliferation of denominations—different types of churches— should be resisted on principle.

In practice this meant that once a "national church" had been established, different peoples who lived within that nation were left to be evangelized by their countrymen.

Winter pointed out that national boundaries were often artificial constructions that included different peoples who were furthest removed from each other culturally, separated by language, social organization, and status—as different as Hindu Brahmins from Boston Brahmins. In fact, Hindu Brahmins were so different culturally from other castes in India, like the Dalits (untouchables), that they were more open to being evangelized by Westerners than other castes. Like it or not, this was simply the case.

Looking through the distorting lens of national churches, 83 percent of the world's non-Christians had become effectively invisible to the missions community. (This is why the term "hidden peoples" was initially used for "unreached peoples.")

Winter said that he had grown up with similarly misleading assumptions. He saw cultural differences among nations as a nuisance and the lack of homogeneity within his own culture as a positive evil. Winter had long awaited the time when everyone, whether black, Chicano, or an Asian emigrant, would worship in places and ways with which he was familiar. But he had since thought better of this. He now saw the church and its various expressions as a grand orchestra. People should not be invited into the church and all commanded to play the violin. Rather, they should be invited to come and play their own instruments— worshiping in a way that fit their own social customs—as long as everyone played from the score of God's word.

Winter pointed out that it was never his intention to exclude anyone for any reason from a given church. He thought that our unity in Christ should not be equated, though, with uniformity in worship and lifestyle.

He based his argument largely on Paul's mission to the Gentiles. Paul, as the first "cross-cultural missionary," was all things to all men that he might win some. He argued continually in his epistles for the freedom of the Greek churches to continue in their own way of life, countering the "Judaizers" who tried to persuade the Greek Christians that they must adopt Jewish customs.

Winter developed an interesting parallel between the question of meat eating in the New Testament and the contemporary situation in India. The Greeks felt free to eat meat (offered to idols) while Jewish Christians thought this an abomination. Paul defended the freedom of the Greeks to eat meat while counseling them not to exercise it in a scandalous way. Winter pointed out that Indian Brahmins who became Christians might remain reluctant to eat meat—since their caste practiced vegetarianism—while most Christians in India included meat in their diet. Why not allow Brahmins to have a church of their own where they would not be under pressure to renounce their traditional dietary habits?

In the most passionate moments of Dr. Winter's speech, he pressed the point home. If God gathered the whole world into a single congregation Sunday after Sunday, there would inevitably be a great loss of the Christian tradition's rich diversity. "Does God want this?" Winter asked. "Do we want this? *Christ died for these people* ... He didn't die to make Muslims stop praying five times a day or to make Brahmins eat meat. Can't we hear Paul the evangelist say that we must go to these people within the system in which they operate? This is the cry of a cross-cultural evangelist."

Winter finished with a charge to the congress: "We must have radically new efforts of cross-cultural evangelism in order to effectively witness to these twenty-three hundred eighty-seven million [2.387 billion] people. And we cannot believe that we should continue virtually to ignore this highest priority." [1]

---

1   For the full text of the speech, see Ralph D. Winter, "The Highest Priority: Cross-Cultural Evangelism," in *Let the Earth Hear His Voice: International Congress on World Evangelization, Lausanne, Switzerland,* ed. J. D. Douglas (Minneapolis: World Wide, 1975), 213ff.

With this declaration and the crashing waves of applause it received throughout the world, Ralph Winter became the most renowned theoretician of evangelical missions.

Most who know about Ralph Winter remember this moment in his life.

More than a few make the mistake of presuming it his greatest achievement.

Standing at the podium in Lausanne, Winter was only on the cusp of the most interesting and productive period of his life. Everything that had come before would turn out to be only a preparation for the huge risks he would soon take in service of what he had called "this highest priority." As he often pointed out, the speech he gave at Lausanne was as much the product of his colleagues' thinking as his own.

Winter's years of experience and study had yet to coalesce into his fully mature understanding of the Christian faith itself. He had applied his inventive, scientific mind to many of the organizational and technical challenges faced by evangelical missions, but he had yet to grasp fully the mission at Christianity's core and its implications for the world's greatest intellectual challenges and practical problems. His fully mature thinking, which came surprisingly late in life, sketches out a road map for the Christian movement's direction in the twenty-first century, just as his remarks at Lausanne influenced the final years of the twentieth. Just as Winter was unafraid to risk his reputation to challenge conventional thinking in order to turn the world of missiology upside down at Lausanne, so he would boldly challenge made-up minds on theology in his later years.

At Lausanne, the drama of Winter's life might be said only to have begun. At Lausanne he had risked criticism and disagreement. When he struck out in new theological directions a few years later, he put the meaning of his life at risk and soon faced ridicule, active opposition, and even vicious, personal attacks. Yet Winter was a visionary who sought to wed pragmatism with truth, even at great personal cost. He believed that the success of the kingdom of God was of paramount importance.

The story of Ralph Winter's life, which provides a wonderful basis for examining his thinking, was a long, adventure-filled process of discovery, with the California engineer always ready to ask probing questions and follow wherever the evidence led. It began much in the way it ended, with a boy who influenced everyone around him and was always recruiting people into his plans.

BANG FOR THE BUCK

As children, Ralph and his brothers liked fireworks. Their father Hugo helped Ralph and his older brother, Paul, to order fireworks from a catalog once a year. The sheer pleasure of Roman candles, bottle rockets, Black Cats, cherry bombs, and M-80s wasn't enough for Ralph. His brother Paul and he pooled their allowance and based their order on calculations that "maximized the bang for their buck," as Ralph remembered. He then thought of ways of improving on their "return on investment" through engineering the brand goods into homemade pyrotechnics—early experiments that "nearly killed him," according to Paul. He was "very competitive," Paul said. "Whatever he did, he really had the ability of seeing right through to the basic principles."

His younger brother, David, saw him the same way. "Ralph was deeply curious about life … He was an experimenter and inventor. He always had a better way to do it. There was hardly anything he didn't think he could improve."

Throughout his life Ralph would approach the stock goods of others' thinking in the same way he did standard-issue fireworks, grasping first principles that allowed him to reengineer ideas with explosive results, some of which "nearly killed him"—or at least his reputation in the eyes of others.

Ralph's influence on others, as his brothers' comments indicate, stemmed from his pleasure in ideas as solutions to problems—

often problems others failed to see. The compelling power of a new idea gave this otherwise introverted figure an unlikely charisma.

That was one side of Ralph Winter. The other side, less spectacular if even more unusual, was his trust in God. Like many of the celebrated heroes of the faith, like the saints of tradition, Ralph had a preternatural faith from his early years. The Scriptures tell us faith is a gift, and as there are degrees of giftedness in other areas, there are as to faith as well.

Ralph expressed it this way: "I early caught on to the fact that I could learn more, learn faster and retain longer by directly concerning myself with the concerns of God for his kingdom and for his righteousness. That is to say, I was an early believer. The will of God in this imperfect world was central early in my thinking." [2]

How many can say that the "will of God in this imperfect world" was their personal key to learning? This is exceedingly rare.

Not only rare but curious, because while the will of God helped Ralph understand the world around him, its application to his own life was elusive. For a long period Ralph was a whirlwind of activity in search of a vocation.

His parents gave him a solid Christian upbringing. From his mother, born Hazel Clare Patterson, Ralph received much of his intelligence, his unpretentious nature, his wit, and his lifelong respect for the abilities of women. Born on Christmas Day, 1894 in Chicago, Illinois, Hazel Clare was outgoing and highly intelligent. Her greatest disappointment was in not being able to finish college. Hazel's father worked as an engineer overseeing the installation of icehouses for a Chicago-based company, and the Patterson family moved to a different city around the country roughly every two years during Hazel's youth.

2   Ralph D. Winter, *Frontiers in Mission: Discovering and Surmounting Barriers to the Missio Dei* (Pasadena, California: William Carey International University Press, 2008), 1.

Despite this, Hazel became the statewide president of the coed Christian Endeavor movement in Arizona. Christian Endeavor was a youth ministry that provided faith formation and leadership skills in local churches. Its members designed and ran the meetings themselves. Hazel's statewide presidency coincided with the suffrage movement's advocacy of the vote for women. Although no social revolutionary, Hazel Winter would always insist that the role of women in any endeavor not be denigrated—a lesson her son took to heart.

The Christian Endeavor youth movement would remain important throughout Hazel's life, and it was at a Christian Endeavor youth camp sponsored by the Presbyterian Church in Hollenbeck Heights, California, that Ralph's father, Hugo, and she would meet. They were married on New Year's Day, 1913.

Known in later life as "Mr. Freeway," Ralph's father was a quiet, largely self-educated man whose accomplishments always spoke for him. He showed Ralph and his other sons how much could be learned on one's own and how much could be accomplished through diligence, honesty, patient endurance, and good humor. No one in the Winter family ever remembered their father becoming angry with their mother. Ralph would later display a similar placidity when everyone around him thought it was time to panic.

Hugo was the youngest son of a butcher who had emigrated to the U.S. from eastern Germany in the 1860s. After graduating from high school, he completed a two-year engineering program at a polytechnic school. Then he married and served in Belgium and France during World War I. He remained in the Army Reserve, rising to the position of captain.

After the war, he began working for the City of Los Angeles as a mechanical draftsman. He worked his way up through the ranks of the L.A. Planning Department until he became head of bridge building in 1936. He went on to supervise some twelve hundred engineers in the Rapid Transit and Design division. Quiet man though he was, he earned the nickname "Mr. Freeway" by obtaining the cooperation of seventy-seven different municipalities as Los Angeles began building its landmark freeway system—a work in progress that has yet to complete the original design envisioned by Hugo's department.

After his compulsory retirement from the Planning Department, the city created the Metropolitan Transportation Engineering Board so that Hugo could go on spearheading work on the city's freeway system for another ten years. He also became a part-time instructor at the University of Southern California's School of Engineering. Hugo provided his family with a highly stable home life. This was particularly valued by his wife, Hazel, who had moved so often during her own childhood, and it set a pattern that Ralph maintained even in the midst of far-flung missionary adventures.

Hugo and Hazel's second son, Ralph Dana Winter, came into the world December 8, 1924, in Los Angeles, two and a half years after the eldest son, Paul. His birth was a difficult one, and the birth of the third son, David, was not until six years later for that reason. Ralph was small in stature and sometimes unwell, suffering what he called "normal" febrile convulsions as a young child. He liked being alone and was a very intense child with perfectionist tendencies.

The Winters were a God-centered, evangelical family during a time of religious change in America. A wing of the Presbyterian church became increasingly involved in the "social gospel," recasting traditional doctrine with an eye to social concerns. Early in their married life, Hugo and Hazel found themselves in what Ralph described as a "fairly liberal" church, Highland Park Presbyterian. Nevertheless, Ralph gave his life to Christ there, when "a chalk-talk evangelist somehow got in the Sunday School."[3]

---

3   Winter, *Frontiers*, 1.

Hazel found herself ill at ease with Highland Park's social pretensions and its college-professor-type airs. She reminded her sons that there was little value in learning to be "cultured" for the sake of status.

When Highland Park found itself too cultured for Christian Endeavor in 1935, the Winters found a new church home, Lake Avenue Congregational Church in Pasadena. This would be Ralph's church home for most of the rest of his life. (Ralph and Roberta attended Glendale Presbyterian Church for approximately fifteen years in the '70s and '80s, where Roberta served as an elder.)

Similarly, the Winter home at 533 Hermosa Street in South Pasadena would be his anchor. Until almost the end of his life Ralph had the same phone number he had as a boy, having inherited the property as an adult.

His parents did not shelter him. He was allowed to think and act for himself and encountered his share of danger, as attested to by his firecracker experiments. He remembers at one time having to alter his usual route home from school in order to avoid an older boy who was bullying him. While in junior high, he was in class when he heard the gunshots fired by a lunatic school principal who killed five teachers, including a science teacher who was one of Ralph's favorites.

Ralph worked at various jobs as a boy, including newspaper delivery and selling and delivering the *Saturday Evening Post*. Even in these ventures he looked to improve the way things were done. He began selling Christmas cards by asking, "Do you want to buy some Christmas cards?" Repeated turndowns prompted a new approach. "Would you like to see some Christmas cards?" he'd ask. Almost everyone said yes, and many then bought the ones they liked.

He was known from the beginning to think and act distinctly from those around him. He never felt compelled to be like anyone else or do things the same way. In an interview later in life, Paul described the young Ralph as "being from somewhere else."

He remembered that Ralph came to the conclusion that every Christian ought to be able to play the piano for the purpose of accompanying chorus and hymn singing. Instead of taking lessons, Ralph checked out books on piano theory and basic chords and taught himself. He developed skill on the clarinet to an even greater extent, playing in the junior high marching band, even mastering "Flight of the Bumblebee." He gave it up, however, after reading Foxe's *Book of Martyrs,* deciding to live a simple "wartime" lifestyle.

Like their parents before them, both the older Winter boys were involved in Christian Endeavor, which contributed substantially to the leadership ability Ralph would exhibit throughout his life.

Later in his adolescence, Ralph also involved himself with another Christian movement, the Navigators, along with his lifelong friend, Dan Fuller, whom he met in high school. Dan was the son of Charles E. Fuller, host of the popular radio programs *The Pilgrim Hour* and *The Old Fashioned Revival Hour* on the Mutual Broadcasting System. Both Dan and Ralph had been involved in Christian Endeavor, and the two together became part of a Bible study group called Dunamis—a name based on the Greek word meaning "power" or "might."

Dunamis groups met in homes, including the Winters' home, once Ralph and Paul joined. Through this group, Ralph memorized some five hundred Bible verses and Dan Fuller more than one thousand. Ralph's daughter, Beth Winter Gill, reported finding toward the end of her father's life a box in his garage containing these verses—the experience had been that treasured.

Through his high-school Navigators experience, Ralph first encountered the movement's founder, Dawson Trotman. Trotman asked a memorable question that became a lens through which Ralph examined his own life. "Why am I doing what I am doing," Trotman asked, "the way I am doing it?"

Trotman also lived by this motto: "Don't do what others can do or will do if there are things to be done that others can't do or won't do."

Trotman became the young Winter's oracle, and these memorable quotations turned into puzzlers as Winter investigated many paths to few personal conclusions. He threw himself into every opportunity for Christian service that presented itself. He even investigated other faiths, reading *The Book of Mormon* and texts on Eastern religions, an enterprise that horrified his mother. Nothing ever affected his trust in Christ. Was there a task, though, that others couldn't or wouldn't do that he should consider his own?

The restlessness he felt in his youth, and his dissatisfaction with what he was taught and the way he was taught it, shows up in a statement he made at seventy-eight years of age: "In our society the unbending social consensus, the pervasive conviction, is that, in order to grow up right, during their first twenty-four years, people need to be incarcerated in little square rooms and battered over the head with books full of facts irrelevant at that age." He characterized these years as "typically unprofitable."[4]

Ralph Winter would earn a PhD in his first "unprofitable" twenty-nine years. Most would consider that a fairly good start. Ralph did not, because he was still so far from finding his place. He had not come close to answering the question: "Why am I doing what I am doing in the way that I am doing it?"

Others noticed his restlessness and feared he would become a failure. Even his family, while supportive, sometimes despaired of his finding direction.

Events in the greater world soon gave everyone marching orders, however. When Ralph graduated from high school in 1942, America was six months into the Second World War.

---

4   Ibid.

A WARTIME LIFESTYLE

The Japanese attack on Pearl Harbor took place on December 7, 1941, the day before Ralph Winter's seventeenth birthday. A high school senior, Winter would be too young to enlist for another full year. Graduating in June of 1942, he followed in his brother's footsteps and enrolled at Caltech for the fall semester. He then enlisted in the Navy in early 1943, expecting to be called up after completing his freshman year at Caltech.

The following summer of 1943 marked the beginning of his lifelong dedication to the cause of Christian missions. Winter accompanied a group of young people—mainly college girls—to Oaxaca, Mexico, to observe the work of various missionaries sponsored by the Lake Avenue Church. Winter's future wife, Roberta, tells us that young Ralph was asked along for the purpose of changing tires should that become necessary! That trip, plus a series of Sunday night talks by missionaries at Lake Avenue, made an impression on the young Winter that would eventually lead him into his life's work. Foreign missions presented many opportunities that would go wanting but for those who were completely dedicated to God's kingdom, as Winter desired to be.

When Winter was called to service later that summer, the Navy was frantically building airfields and bases across the Pacific Rim, and engineers were urgently needed. Because Winter was already an engineering student, the Navy sent him back to Caltech following boot camp. There he would finish his civil engineering education at government expense through an accelerated program where three years of study would be crammed into eighteen months.

By the fall of 1943, the Navy also had an urgent need for pilots, and put out a service-wide request for qualified trainees for the Naval Air Corps. Winter wanted to volunteer, but with two semesters still to go at Caltech and preflight school to begin in January, he would not be eligible. Or would he? He saw no reason not to finish his degree in time to start flight school. In what became his inimitable style, he sought and was granted permission to take his last two Caltech semesters simultaneously.

That September Winter began a gruesome double classload followed by fifteen three-hour exams during the final two weeks. With the kind of dedication he was to show throughout his life, he completed the two-in-one semester, passing his courses and making himself eligible to begin flight school. No other Caltech student has ever done—before or since—what Winter did that semester in 1944.

August of 1945 saw the Japanese surrender and the end of the war. At the time, Ralph Winter was an air cadet in the Navy's V-6 fighter training program at Saint Mary's preflight school. Winter and others in his circumstances were transferred to inactive duty, a move that left him free to go home and resume his former life. His flight training remained incomplete, but he was unencumbered by the massive discharge program that would leave most other servicemen on active duty for months following the war. While he never flew during his time in the Navy, Winter's service was to pay off handsomely. The Navy had already paid for most of his undergraduate training at Caltech, leaving him debt-free.

While most Caltech graduates would have moved quickly into a career, Winter was just beginning to prepare for whatever God wanted him to do. He had little money, and most universities had closed out fall registration. Winter turned to his trusted pastor, Dr. James Henry Hutchins, for guidance.

Hutchins knew of Winter's interest in biblical studies and suggested courses in Bible and Greek at Westmont College, where Hutchins was a board member. Westmont had been a Christian liberal arts college in the Los Angeles area. It had just sold its Los Angeles property and purchased adjoining estates in the beautiful foothills above Santa Barbara, where it planned to establish a new campus.

The school's board members were determined to begin the 1945–46 academic year in the two newly purchased mansions, and the change in campus delayed the opening of fall classes until October. Winter still had time to enroll and was immediately accepted.

Without the means to pay tuition, Winter took what he did have—his previous education and experience—and used these as barter. For legal reasons, Westmont needed to have a survey done and a topographical map made of the new campus. As a civil engineer, Winter knew that he could produce both, if provided with a team of assistants. The school also needed someone to teach remedial math, where Winter could also supply the bill. He approached the school with the idea that he teach both the remedial math course and a course in surveying in exchange for tuition. Westmont agreed.

Four students, all early-release veterans like Winter, enrolled in his course. Winter set about teaching these students surveying through developing the survey and map Westmont needed. Soon they became accomplished assistants. Learning by doing would become one of Ralph's trademark pedagogical methods. (All four student assistants, it turned out, were destined for the mission field, and several reported to him in later years that their course in surveying had helped them in their overseas work.)

Winter enrolled in the Greek and Bible courses, and also in a course in church history, a subject he had been interested in since the age of fifteen.

Dr. Elbert McCleary, a retired missionary, taught the course in New Testament Greek using an oral method. A true linguist, McCleary was convinced that no language could be learned effectively unless it was taught orally and spoken by the students. Without being able to speak a language, even a classical language, a person's understanding of the language would always be inferior.

That was Dr. McCleary's principle, and it was also the principle of the Army Language Training Program taught in Monterey, California. There, as Dr. McCleary knew, the Army was teaching conversational ability in foreign languages over a matter of months rather than years. McCleary believed that the same method was needed to teach biblical languages in order that they be understood properly.

Winter was immediately impressed by this methodology. Like McCleary, he saw the value in understanding a language by speaking it conversationally. He already believed that students should learn biblical Greek by speaking it, the way the Apostle Paul did in the first century.

Despite his experience in Christian Endeavor and the Navigators' Bible verse memory program, Winter had never taken a formal Bible study course before enrolling at Westmont. Westmont's course introduced him to the inductive method of Bible study, a departure from the deductive approach in which other studies and texts are used to explain Bible passages. With the inductive method, students would read the biblical text, asking first, "What does it *say?*" without referring to scholarly interpretation. The next step was to ask, "What does the text *mean?*" and then, finally, "What does this *mean to my life?*" Only then should the student consult other studies to see what others believe the passage meant.

The book *Methodical Bible Study* describes the contrast of the two approaches:

Deduction ... begins with generalization and moves for their support to the particulars. By its very nature, deduction tends to be subjective and prejudicial ... induction is objective and impartial, for it demands that one first examine particulars of the Scriptures and that one's conclusions be based on those particulars. Such an approach is sound, because, being objective, it corresponds to the objective nature of the Scriptures. [5]

The reasoning may be fallacious, but what's being described here as inductive Bible study allows Scripture to speak first to the heart before the student becomes entangled in scholarship. It certainly brought the power of the Scriptures home to the young Ralph Winter.

The Westmont course was taught by a woman who had studied under Howard Tilman Kuist at Biblical Seminary in New York, where the method had originated. Kuist had written a book, *These Words Upon My Heart,* focusing on careful Bible study with an emphasis on character development for believers.

Winter was taken with the Inductive Bible Study (IBS) concept. As with so many things, he shared his new passion for IBS with his good friend Dan Fuller, who also became enamored of the method. As Fuller later described it in the Fuller Theological Seminary newsletter:

This method is characterized as "Inductive" because the procedure involves a mastery of the particulars of the Bible text before coming to any general conclusions as to its meaning. By the particulars is meant the basic data of the text, stripped of all interpretive aids that men have added. Hence we are not bound to the punctuation, versification, paragraphing or chapter divisions. In fact we

---

5   Robert A. Traina, *Methodical Bible Study: A New Approach to Hermeneutics* (New York: Biblical Seminary in New York, 1952), 7.

must go behind the English translation to that text in the
original which represents the best results of textual criticism to find the starting point for the inductive method. [6]

Winter took the concept of IBS in a number of different directions. He envisioned the idea of taking a "motion picture" approach
to teaching the Bible visually, which would be a way of exciting
people about getting into a serious study of the Bible. As he
described it, "You could teach the book of Matthew in an hour
and people would learn more than in a year-long Sunday School
study." As was so often the case in Ralph Winter's life, his innovative mind took him out in front of accepted methodology, which
often annoyed professors and administrators. Frequently his ideas
were simply not taken seriously because of his age and lack of
credentials. He would tuck his ideas away, though, for future use.

At the end of the school year, Winter found himself facing two
options for further study: basic linguistics, which he envisioned
might lead to writing on how to teach Greek through immersive
conversation, and a dedicated study of the Bible using the inductive approach. He decided on the Bible study.

Learning that Howard Tilman Kuist had transferred to
Princeton Theological Seminary, Winter was certain that he
should go there as well. He convinced Dan Fuller to join him,
and both enrolled at Princeton as special students for one year
of study in the fall of 1946.

There were two obstacles to the young men's attending
Princeton. One was parental objection: Princeton had recently
become a far more liberal institution, biblically speaking, than in
past years. A new administration had shifted the school's emphasis
from historical Calvinism to twentieth-century Barthianism,

---

6 Letter from D.P. Fuller to Alumni regarding inductive Bible study, *Theology News and
Notes* 2:4, 1995, 6–9, quoted in Greg Howard Parsons, "Ralph D. Winter's Life and Legacy:
Missiology, Vision and Strategy" (unpublished PhD dissertation, University of Wales, 2009
draft), 36.

with its subjective understanding of the inspiration of Scripture, as the text "becomes" the word of God when accepted as such by the hearer in the context of a believing community. Traditional Calvinism taught that the Scriptures were the inspired word of God, however sinful men and women might view them. While Winter and Fuller were aware of the controversy, both had a clear focus on developing their knowledge of Inductive Bible Study, and each felt the other could keep him accountable and not let him stray from the Bible as his final authority of faith and practice while at Princeton.

The second obstacle was tuition, and this was immediately overcome by the enactment that very year of the G.I. Bill, which enabled those who had served in the war to receive college tuition credits courtesy of the United States government. The bill would pay the cost of tuition and textbooks, plus $75 per month, to any veteran who wished to attend college or graduate school. Because of the G.I. Bill and a similar program enacted by the state of California, Winter was to survive all his postgraduate studies debt free.

When Winter enrolled at Princeton in 1946 at age twenty-one, he hoped only to better prepare himself to serve God as a layman. He had no intention of finishing a seminary education or becoming ordained, as he felt that kind of call should come only from a church body. To be a minister was a special calling, one he suspected he did not have. By developing his deep interest in the Bible and biblical language teaching methods, he hoped to serve God's kingdom as well or better than he could by becoming a minister.

The year at Princeton went well for Winter and for Dan Fuller. Both were fascinated by the inductive study of the Bible as taught by Dr. Kuist.

Returning home to Pasadena the following summer, the two essentially took over the college department Sunday school at Lake Avenue Church, where they taught the books of Matthew and Luke using the inductive method. While Winter moved into other fields afterwards, Dan Fuller made teaching the Bible his life's work, becoming a professor in that field at the seminary founded by his father.

While at Princeton, Winter also attended the first "Urbana" Student Missionary Conference in Toronto, Canada, between Christmas and New Year's Day, along with J. Christy Wilson, the InterVarsity Christian Fellowship representative for the Princeton campus, and several other students. This conference, put on by InterVarsity, brought together almost five hundred and seventy-five students from fifty-two denominations to hear speakers such as Robertson C. McQuilkin, president of Columbia Bible College; Harold Ockenga of Park Street Congregational Church in Boston; L. E. Maxwell of the Prairie Bible Institute in Alberta, Canada; and some of North America's most influential missionaries. (One result of the conference would be the formation of a similar mission conference at Princeton by Winter and Wilson. Among the conference speakers Ralph would enlist were world-renowned New Testament scholar, Bruce Metzger, and Eugene Nida, a linguistic expert. As he would do so often, Winter was already bringing together key individuals in order to help them enhance their own contributions to the needs of world missions.)

To save the cost of riding to Toronto with the other students, Winter chose to make use of a skill he had picked up while in the service, and hitchhiked alone from New Jersey. Dressed inadequately, he encountered snow that was five feet deep along the roadsides.

Once in Toronto, he bought a heavy jacket from a street peddler for $25. The purchase, and other expenses, left him a princely thirty-five cents for his hitchhike home after the conference.

On the way back, he had to pay five cents just to be allowed to cross the Niagara Falls bridge, and another five cents to get from the western outskirts of Syracuse to the eastern side of the city, where he hoped to get a ride toward New York. Down to twenty-five cents and standing in falling sleet, his suitcase over his head, Winter got a ride as far as Schenectady, then another to New York City. Dropped off at the George Washington Bridge in New Jersey, he found himself at night in falling snow still one hundred miles from Princeton. A driver miraculously stopped for him in the 10 p.m. dark. Ralph was broke, wet, cold, and looked like a hobo in his street-peddler jacket. Nevertheless, the driver took him all the way to Princeton and dropped him at his dormitory door at just past midnight!

His late arrival back at Princeton led to one of Ralph's many initiatives. Instead of being sleepy, he must have been exhilarated by having survived the ordeal. Entering the dormitory, he picked up a copy of *United Evangelical Action,* the official magazine of the National Association of Evangelicals. Paging through it, he found an intriguing news item. The government of Muslim Afghanistan, for centuries tightly closed to the gospel, was requesting American aid in the form of twenty-two teachers of English. Ralph seized the opportunity this request presented for mission. These teachers could serve Afghan society and be "light and salt" in the world at the same time. He enlisted his Princeton classmate J. Christy Wilson into the challenge as well. Wilson went on to become renowned for his work in Afghanistan—one of the few evangelicals ever to be accepted and even revered in that country. Winter thought he would go to Afghanistan himself one day, but first turned his attention to recruiting others.

That next fall, having finished their year at Princeton, Winter, Dan Fuller, and their friend Bill Bright enrolled at Fuller Theological Seminary back in Pasadena. The school had just been started by Charles Fuller (Dan's father) and by Dr. Harold Ockenga, who had been one of the speakers at the Urbana conference.

While Winter had plans to work on a primer for teaching Greek during his off hours, his father had different ideas. Hugo Winter was a believer in self-sufficiency and thought that if Ralph, now twenty-two years old, was going to be living at home, he needed to have a job to pay for his upkeep. Ralph had worked odd jobs since his boyhood. Most of his education had been paid for by the U.S. Navy and the G.I. Bill, with Ralph making up shortfalls with his own earnings. He had worked as an engineering drafts-man the summer before his first year at Caltech, and later as an engineer both in Pasadena and New Jersey.

As he began his studies at Fuller, however, the only job Winter could find was as a dishwasher in a drive-in restaurant. The need to take this job, while Ralph's pet project of developing a Greek primer went undone, brought Ralph into conflict with his parents. His own sense of leadership was developing, even as his respect for his father remained strong. At first he yielded, only because he had to in order to live at home. Later he realized that he had to put his own priorities aside; that it was right to yield to his father's authority, and that, where his son was concerned, his father had the right to be wrong. Washing dishes became a part of God's work and of God's plan for Ralph Winter. He never flinched at manual labor or any other type of menial work, which helped later when he was put in charge of a compost heap as a missionary.

While at Fuller that year, Winter explored the issue of faith and science. As Roberta would write years later, Ralph "continued to learn things not taught in secular schools about the relationship of the story of the Faith and the unfolding of Western civilization." Caltech had prided itself on including biography and history in its science curriculum, claiming that its BS degree included all the learning available in other schools' BA degrees. While there, Winter had learned about the lives of great scientists such as Isaac Newton, Michael Faraday, William Thompson (Lord Kelvin), James Clark, and Sir Humphrey Davy. But it was not until he discovered a book called *Five Men of Science* while at Princeton that he realized that Caltech had totally ignored what to four of the five was even more important than their scientific achievements—that is, their Christian faith. A proper study of these men's lives revealed that it was their faith that had led them into scientific discovery. The God of creation, they were convinced, had to be a God of order; and if that were true, he intended for us to find and understand that order. This insight had a tremendous impact on Winter, who, according to Roberta, "considered this a second conversion, a conversion 'back' to science and [he] carried this discovery with him into his first year at Fuller." [7]

So another project formed in Ralph's imagination: He would teach an off-campus course to students at secular colleges and universities that would incorporate God into their scientific curriculum. In short, he would become a history teacher to Christian students in secular schools, beginning with those at the nearby University of Southern California (USC).

While Winter quickly realized that he was not qualified to be a history teacher, he knew there were students at Fuller who might be. He surveyed the fifty students who made up Fuller's first class, looking for history majors. Two had excelled in history at evan-

---

7 Roberta H. Winter, "Winter Initiatives" (unpublished document, Pasadena, September 31, 2000), 20.

gelical Wheaton College. They had even used the same textbook as
the students at USC. Here was the connection he thought he was
looking for. What, he asked, had the Wheaton professors added to
the textbook from a Christian perspective? The surprising answer
was "nothing." These students had no more insight into Winter's
questions than would students from secular colleges. What's more,
they had no interest in helping with Ralph's project.

Winter took it upon himself to read all he could regarding the
impact of the Christian movement on every historical period, and
he organized and led a weekly, off-campus night class for five USC
InterVarsity students. The class was more of an experiment than
anything else, and only lasted one semester. The idea of an integrated curriculum that treated history from a Christian perspective
stayed with the twenty-two-year-old, however—long enough to
consume the decade of his seventies.

During their year at Fuller Seminary, Winter, Fuller, and
several other young men began studying the history of Christian
revivals and began praying that God would touch the Lake
Avenue Church with a revival of its own. (Winter had experienced a revival at Westmont College during the summer of 1946
that had been initiated by the chapel talk of a retired missionary.)
As the idea of what the young men were after became known,
most of the Lake Avenue Church members were horrified. What
excesses might a revival produce? Dr. Hutchins was disturbed
at what they were doing, and Dan's parents—paradoxically, the
founders of *The Old Fashioned Revival Hour* radio program—were
also concerned. Their patrician breeding made them suspect of
too much emotion. Worse, Dan had taken up an interest in simple
living and was reading all he could about it. The Fullers thought
they were losing their son to fanaticism and blamed Ralph.

During the summer of 1948, Winter continued to pursue his interest in languages and went to Norman, Oklahoma, to the Wycliffe Summer Institute of Linguistics. His interest was both in finding effective ways of learning foreign languages to facilitate mission work and to meet the global need to teach English. Linguistics seemed to him the key to his dual interest in language teaching and Bible study. The Wycliffe course was designed for missionaries going to unreached tribal peoples. It strengthened both of his interests and introduced him to people who were to become leaders in the linguistics field. This course of study, more than any other, set him on the path to majoring in linguistics for his graduate degrees. While at the Wycliffe course Ralph would persuade Eugene Nida, a Wycliffe instructor and later the translation secretary of the American Bible Society, to give a side seminar on a scientific analysis of New Testament Greek. In 1950, when Nida wrote his doctoral dissertation on the linguistic analysis of English, Winter single-handedly reproduced a number of copies that he sold at cost. Later, Winter's own PhD dissertation dissected a similar field, again based on the modern study of descriptive linguistics, backed by advanced mathematical formulas of his own conception.

In the fall of 1948, Winter, still only twenty-three years old, returned for his second year at Fuller Seminary. He still had no intention of becoming a minister, wanting only to become a better-informed layman.

Always the initiator, Winter saw his second year at Fuller as a chance to teach Greek by the oral method for an entire academic year, and proposed the idea to Dr. Gleason Archer, the newly arrived Greek instructor. Archer did not share Winter's enthusiasm for the project and did not see any reason to risk the seminary's reputation on what he considered a harebrained idea. Undismayed, Winter took his idea to the president of nearby Pasadena Nazarene College, where Koine Greek was also taught. He was introduced to the Greek professor, Dr. Mayfield, who agreed to let him try it, with the understanding that anyone taking Winter's course would also have to take and pass Dr. Mayfield's final exam. And, of course, Winter would not be paid any salary.

Eight students enrolled in Winter's class before he had developed the course. He worked endless hours, producing basic diagrams and learning techniques from scratch. Taking a full class load at Fuller and teaching Greek to eight Pasadena Nazarene College students was like taking the two semesters in one at Caltech. The difficulty involved in constantly developing the Greek course led eventually to his dropping some classes at Fuller during the second semester. Teaching had to be the priority: he had to teach eight students enough Greek to pass Dr. Mayfield's exam!

Although his students were learning to speak Greek, Winter realized by midterm that speaking the language wasn't going to help them pass the exam Dr. Mayfield let him preview. The Apostle Paul couldn't have passed, Ralph thought. Reluctantly, he began incorporating more traditional content into the course, and at year's end all of his eight students passed, but just barely.

To the end of his life, Winter believed in the oral method of teaching biblical languages. At one point in his career he suggested to a student of Hebrew that he should live in Israel for a couple of years. He later learned that the young man did so and never regretted it, becoming an Old Testament professor in one of America's well-known seminaries.

That summer of 1949, Winter, now twenty-four years old, still had no clear idea of what to do with his life and talents. Having the summer free, following the pressure-filled school year, and learning that the Linguistic Society of America was going to hold its annual Institute of Linguistics at the University of Michigan in Ann Arbor, he registered to attend. This meeting, and an additional course offered by Dr. Charles C. Fries and Dr. Robert Lado, two top professors in the field of Teaching English as a Second Language (TESL), stoked the fire of his enthusiasm for language, linguistics, and how the human mind acquires a language.

As the summer ended, Winter needed to find a place for himself in the fall, and now his other interest—new methodologies for teaching the Bible—again commanded his attention. While at the InterVarsity Christian Fellowship (IVCF) convention in Toronto, he had heard Dr. L. E. Maxwell, president of the Prairie Bible Institute (PBI) in Three Hills, Alberta, speak. Although put off by Maxwell's style of preaching, Winter remembered hearing from a Princeton classmate of how that classmate's brother, a United Church of Christ (Canada) pastor, had taken a course on the Gospel of John from the small, nonaccredited school and found it so powerful that he returned for more education. As a result of his Prairie Bible Institute studies, this young pastor had come to know the Lord in a new and personal way.

With his evangelical background and his education at both a "liberal" seminary and a "conservative" one, Winter was intrigued. What was it, he wondered, that could have such an effect on an ordained minister? And, closer to Winter's main interest, how was this place teaching the Bible? He enrolled for the fall semester.

Prairie Bible Institute used a teaching technique that might be called "group inductive study," through which students were given sets of search questions to be answered after an assigned Bible passage was read. After answering the questions, students then wrote down any insights on the subject picked up in class and from other students. They were ultimately graded on their own answers and the group's.

Winter was there for only a single semester. His trip home that winter was a miserable one. He and several other students, wrapped in blankets for warmth, drove an unheated car through a continual snowstorm. When they stopped to warm up at a roadside restaurant in Montana, the precious blankets were stolen, making the trip south almost unbearable. But this one semester made a vast contribution to his future as a teacher and missionary. He was so impressed by the teaching methodology that he would later adapt it to the history classes he would teach at Fuller Seminary, and ultimately through his World Christian Foundations curriculum. And he would also find that his PBI studies contributed to his credibility as an educator. As a teacher at the School for World Mission at Fuller, he would sometimes detect a coolness toward him from students with a more conservative background—a coolness that was almost always replaced by trust when they learned that he had studied at Prairie Bible Institute.

During the spring semester of 1950, Ralph Winter found himself taking no formal course of study for the first time since graduating from high school. He had but one degree, that in civil engineering from Caltech, but during that time, he had taken on study courses that encompassed much of what he would later put together as his life's work. He had researched the Christian influences on history, recruited English teachers for Afghanistan, studied innovative ideas for language learning, researched the history and results of revivals in America, and studied Bible teaching techniques. All this, plus some of the training to become a fighter pilot with the U.S. Navy, though he never actually got into a plane! He had never tried to make a name for himself, often passing on ideas for others to implement. He was an engineer, a designer; others were better equipped for building his conceptions.

During this time off from formal schooling, Winter began to think again of Afghanistan. At this time he was still planning on going there, but thought it important to get a master's degree in Teaching English as a Second Language first; perhaps even a PhD.

Family friend and fellow Lake Avenue Church member, Dick Soderberg, had been to Afghanistan as an engineer and had helped to persuade that country's Ministry of Education to open a technical school—the Afghan Institute of Technology (AIT)—which was modeled roughly after Caltech. His mission now was to get the scientific and technical equipment needed for the school. During Winter's semester off, Soderberg was home recruiting for the new school.

Ralph's brother Paul responded to the opportunity. He and his wife, Betty, would serve two years in Afghanistan, where Paul became president of the school, his position funded by UNESCO. Another Lake Avenue friend, Maynard Eyestone, and his wife also went. Ralph's father, "Mr. Freeway," became the U.S. president of the Afghan Institute of Technology, Inc. This was the corporate entity that Ralph had set up so that companies and schools in the U.S. could donate books and equipment for AIT.

That winter and spring, Ralph lived in a missionary apartment at the Hawthorne Gospel Church in Hawthorne, New Jersey, spending his days calling on technical schools on the East Coast for donations to the effort. As Roberta Winter would later write: "He was certainly not overwhelmed with equipment—nor books—but what he did get enabled the school to get started. For [Ralph], this time was in a real sense a training for him in diplomacy and in working with secular entities." Soderberg continued to recruit teachers for the new school.

By now, friends of the Winter family were increasingly puzzled by all of Ralph's activity and initiative. They began to ask Ralph's mother, "What on earth is Ralph's calling?" They assumed he was becoming a minister when he attended seminary, but now he had dropped out completely. First he was teaching Greek, now he was working for an engineering school in Afghanistan. There seemed to be no cohesiveness, no plan to his life. Family friends believed that Ralph was pursuing such a foggy dream that he'd inevitably end up lost, his talents wasted. His parents stood with him but must have had their own misgivings.

Due to Dick Soderberg, and in large part through the Winter family's initiative, the Afghan Institute of Technology did succeed, though. During the years leading up to the Soviet invasion of Afghanistan, more than one hundred mission-minded people served there either as teachers of English or as engineering professors, both initiatives that Ralph Winter had been key in setting into motion. If Ralph had not as yet become a success in his own right, his projects were starting to demonstrate that his ideas had merit.

While planning to join the others in Afghanistan as a teacher of English, Winter first enrolled at Columbia University Teachers College, at that time the largest school of education in the world. His good friend Maynard Eyestone and another Lake Avenue member joined him there. To say that their budget was limited is an understatement. Starting with a publication Maynard had from the U.S. Department of Agriculture, they used Ralph's slide rule to calculate how they could get the most nutrition out of the least amount of money and still stay healthy. The goal was to achieve at least one hundred calories per penny spent! Ralph would periodically buy powdered milk by the 100 lb. sack off the docks across town, then take it by subway 125 blocks to a station that was five blocks from where they lived. He would walk the five blocks, then carry the sack up five flights of stairs. Meat was scarce—mainly chicken backs and necks for flavor or cooked into casseroles with a protein powder called "Multipurpose Food," made from soy grits. Multipurpose Food had been developed by Clifford Clinton, a former missionary kid in China, who was now wealthy but still interested in feeding the world's poor. A nurse friend of the Lake Avenue trio was concerned about the way they ate. She performed blood tests on the young men and found their hemoglobin was fine, although they needed to include vegetables to stave off minor illnesses.

In June of 1951, Winter received his MA in Teaching English as a Second Language, again in absentia as at Caltech, because he didn't see the need to stick around when he had a cross-country drive to make to get home for the summer—a summer that would hold an unanticipated, life-changing event.

4

THE SCIENCE OF LOVE

Ralph's plans were to spend the summer of 1951 at home in Pasadena, and then to return to Columbia University in the fall to work on a PhD in anthropology.

Because of his involvement as a student leader in Christian Endeavor, and because he had been to seminary, Ralph was invited to speak at a regular session given in the Los Angeles General Hospital chapel. He almost rejected the invitation because of another talk being given later that night at the First Congregational Church of Hollywood. The speaker was Frank Charles Laubach, a Congregationalist missionary and educator, well-known around the world for his teaching methods, which, according to his own estimation, had taught "more than 60 million people speaking two hundred languages and dialects" to read. A thirty-cent postage stamp was later produced to honor his work by the U.S. Postal Service. Ralph was especially interested in one of many books written by Laubach called *The Silent Billion Speak*. Although time would be short, Ralph decided to give his talk and then leave directly to hear Laubach's speech.

And so on July 20 Ralph went to the hospital chapel and spoke to a group of student nurses, including a group of young women from Lake Avenue Congregational Church (LACC). At the conclusion, he asked if any of the young ladies would like to go with him to hear Laubach. He had room for five in his car and that many readily accepted the invitation.

On the way back, several of the very conservative young women stated that they did not believe Laubach to be a real Christian, based less upon what he had said than on the fact that he was a Congregationalist missionary, and had chosen to speak at what was considered a "liberal" church. When Ralph asked the group directly whether they thought Laubach a "real" Christian, only one girl replied yes.

The independent voice belonged to Roberta Helm. She was not technically a part of the LACC group; she came, in fact, from an extremely conservative wing of the Nazarene Church—one which tended to separatism. Partly because of her own strong intuitions, and partly because her religious background emphasized the experiential more than the theological, she was able to sense what kind of person Laubach was. That spiritual perception attracted Ralph. He was especially impressed that, although she came from a narrower background, she was willing to ignore peer pressure in order to state her views. Years later, Roberta would describe the situation in the third person in her publication "Winter Initiatives":

> Among these [young women in the car] was Roberta Helm, a "Nazarene of the Nazarenes," someone said, because she had long hair and was very conscientious in doing what she felt was right. That Ralph would ever become interested in her was not even an option as far as she was concerned. Their theological backgrounds were different. She "looked" different with her long hair, etc. But he had taught for a year at Pasadena (Nazarene) College and had a great respect for Nazarenes.
>
> Also, her obvious unembarrassed willingness to be "different" appealed to him. He had long known that whomever he married would have to be willing not to fit into the usual mold. [8]

---

8   Winter, "Winter Initiatives," 14.

To Roberta's amazement, Ralph asked her out. Of the two, Ralph might have been more surprised. Until that night he thought his vocation might entail celibacy. He had even talked a friend out of marrying in order to devote his life fully to God—Ralph's convictions, at least on his friend's behalf, ran that deep.

Always the engineer, Ralph made a list of things to talk about with Roberta, and on their first date they went through Ralph's list. He must have liked her views because, on their second date, he told her that he thought they should talk seriously about the possibility of getting married! He was to find there would be obstacles. Roberta was not prepared for such an idea. Her family would be opposed to her marrying anyone from a Presbyterian background. After two or three dates, Ralph nearly despaired of marrying Roberta.

Roberta came from a large family with four sisters and two brothers. They had moved from Kansas to south Texas, where her father, Leroy Helm, had been a cowboy and later a leather worker. He was a believer and churchgoing man, but not very interested in study or reading. On the other hand, her mother, Rose Etta, was a godly woman and well read. She was a strong personality and "ruled the roost." The family followed the conservative constraints of the Nazarene Church and had little to do with people of other Christian backgrounds.

With Roberta in mind, Ralph reconsidered his views on marriage. Once, he believed that it was not practical for a dedicated Christian missionary, such as he hoped to be, to marry. He and a handful of like-minded friends had signed a "covenant" titled "Bachelor 'til the Rapture." Now, remarkably, marriage made eminent sense.

Ralph tells us:

> I began to listen to my own self, and I also studied, and
> I realized that most of the Christians in history were
> generated biologically, not evangelistically … and I

> realized that the children of pastors often have a tremen-
> dous advantage and are more influential because of their
> background ... and it's funny to say it like this, but it
> occurred to me again and again that I have the capacity
> to be a husband, to be the husband of a wife. [9]

As so often in his life, Ralph seemed to be approaching the idea
of marriage from an engineering standpoint. But unlike so many
of the other projects he had engineered, he wasn't going to be able
to turn this one over to someone else. During their dating life, he
shared with Roberta his views of frugal living for the Lord. Both
believed in this and would later express their thinking; Ralph in
Reconsecration to a Wartime, Not a Peacetime, Lifestyle; and Roberta
in *The Non-essentials of Life,* in which she tells how Ralph and she
worked through the issue of finances in their marriage and with
their children.

Ralph said goodbye to Roberta and returned to school at
Columbia Teachers College in the fall of 1951. While it had been
his intention to receive a doctorate in anthropology there, he soon
learned that Cornell University, 250 miles away in Ithaca, New
York, offered a PhD program in descriptive languages, his longtime
passion. There, outstanding faculty were researching and teaching
the then-new "structural linguistics" as part of that program.

Ralph called Cornell to register, arranged with the G.I. Bill
campus authority to transfer him, unregistered with Columbia,
packed up, and caught the bus for Ithaca, all within thirty-six
hours! His roommate, Paul Little, was dumbfounded when he
returned to their room and found Ralph and his belongings gone.
(Ralph always regretted that he never got around to apologizing to
him before Paul's death in 1975 in an automobile accident.)

During that fall semester at Cornell, Ralph wrote Roberta a
letter every day for ninety days—some ninety thousand words in

---

9　Interview with Ralph Winter by Greg Parsons on August 7, 2006, 6, quoted in Parsons,
"Ralph D. Winter: Life and Core Missiology," 56.

their estimation. Her interest in him grew as she replied, asking him questions about his beliefs. In his letters, Ralph was trying to persuade Roberta to marry him in spite of her mother's objection that Presbyterians could not be true believers. [10] In her letters, she was testing him to see if he not only believed in sanctification, but also if he actually knew the presence of the Holy Spirit in his heart.

Reunited at semester's end, the two were married at the Bresee Avenue Nazarene Church chapel in Pasadena on December 28. Ralph was twenty-seven, Roberta twenty-two, and they had known each other just five months and one week, three months of which they had spent apart. Ralph and Roberta knew they were made for each other as only two people with such curious yet complementary natures could. They fit instantly like the right jigsaw pieces.

Ralph studied at Cornell for two years, largely under Dr. Charles Hockett, one of the country's foremost linguistic professors, working toward a PhD in descriptive languages with minors in cultural anthropology and mathematical statistics.

His dissertation was typically innovative. Entitled "English Content Words and Function Words: A Quantitative Analysis," it involved, as Roberta described it, "two artificial languages, one combining the vocabulary of the learner's language and the grammar of the foreign language, the other the opposite." [11] Ralph thought that if someone trying to learn a language could use his own vocabulary following the grammar of the new language, and the new language's vocabulary using the grammar of his mother tongue, the student might make far more rapid progress in language acquisition. This theory was backed by statistical formulas that often came to Ralph in the middle of the night.

Roberta helped him with library research and by counting the types of words in three vastly different documents that provided

---

10 Parsons, 2012, 43–45.
11 Winter, "Winter Initiatives," 14.

material for his study. She often sat in on classes with Ralph, and helped support them with part-time nursing jobs. Her assistance during their Cornell years set a lifelong pattern that made Roberta an essential part of Ralph's work. They were always to be a team, working hand in hand.

Before their marriage, Ralph and Roberta had agreed that Roberta should take the Wycliffe Summer Institute of Linguistics course in Norman, Oklahoma, the summer following their first year together in Ithaca. The question of how Ralph would fill his time in Norman was answered when he was accepted by the program director, Kenneth Pike, to teach while Roberta studied.

Ralph's being accepted as a teacher that summer was more important than he realized at the time. During his first year at Cornell, because of his engineering background, Ralph had challenged everything he was taught, even the methods by which he was being taught. He was constantly challenging Dr. Hockett publicly in seminars. Hockett became so frustrated with Winter that he was ready to drop him from the program. He had decided that if Pike, whom he knew and respected, did not hire Ralph to teach that summer, the doctoral candidate would be dropped. Fortunately, Pike brought him on to teach phonemics at the Wycliffe Summer Institute. Ralph went to Norman with Roberta, and she loved every minute of the course work and of her fellowship with the missionaries studying there. Later Ralph would relate that Dr. Hockett believed him to be "bright but without common sense," while he (Winter) thought it was the other way around.

Ralph finished his dissertation in late August of 1953. Until that time, he had not seriously considered entering the ministry, believing he had not been called of the Holy Spirit. Too many ministers were merely careerists, in Ralph's opinion. His exposure to anthropology, however, convinced him that the ministry was,

among other things, a position of credentialed authority. The role
a minister played was recognized almost universally. In many
societies, shamans and priests had a greater ability to bring about
change than even the best qualified laymen. He might never be
able to implement his ideas in service to God's kingdom without
the necessary standing. So he made the decision to complete his
ministerial studies at Princeton Seminary and become ordained
as a Presbyterian minister.

Once again, Winter's decision was made at the very last moment. He had just finished his dissertation in August, so enrolling
at Princeton for the fall semester was practically an impossibility.
Ralph also knew that many of the Princeton professors had a bias
against evangelical (some called them "fundamentalist") students,
of which Ralph was one. Nevertheless, he made his last-minute
application, knowing his chances were slim and put backup plans
in place as well.

Ralph and Roberta moved back to Pasadena where he applied
for a job with the Rand Corporation, a government-related think
tank in Santa Monica. He let the Rand Corporation know that he
was awaiting an answer from Princeton and that he would go there
if accepted. About a week later, he got the good news. Princeton
had a last-minute cancellation and had room for one more student. Within two weeks, Roberta and he boarded a Greyhound
bus for New Jersey, on their way to another three years in Ralph's
educational odyssey. While Ralph's G.I. Bill benefits were running
out, Roberta found nursing work almost immediately. With her
help, he began studying once more.

Ralph soon discovered that, despite its liberal reputation,
Princeton Seminary had plenty of evangelical professors and
staff. Among these was its president, Dr. John McKay, a former
missionary and, according to Roberta, "truly a Godly man." His

son-in-law, Bruce Metzger, head of the Greek department, was another. Dr. McKay had once commented in a chapel address that he would rather have fiery fundamentalists whom he could tone down a bit than to have dead liberals who didn't even know God.

As a seminary student, Ralph would have no time for initiatives. To add to Roberta's nursing income, he found a position as a student pastor at the historic fifty-member Lamington Presbyterian Church thirty miles away. The pay was $100 a month, but included living quarters in the next-door manse. Salary aside, the experience of preaching and administrating a small church would prove invaluable.

Due to his previous two and a half years' seminary experience (one earlier at Princeton and one and a half at Fuller), Winter was admitted as a second-year student, which required a study of first-year Hebrew, a language with which he had no experience. Ralph attended class for a few days, once again became frustrated with the way the class was taught, and took his complaint to the dean. He requested that he be able to learn the language on his own. Because he had a PhD in linguistics, the dean granted permission.

Ralph Winter was now handling the pastoral duties of a small church (including visiting parishioners almost every night) and driving thirty miles to class each day, while studying Hebrew on his own. He could only pray that he would pass the Hebrew exam in the fall. When he and Roberta had their first daughter, Beth, in September, Ralph decided that he would have to stretch his final two years into three to relieve the pressures of time. With Roberta now unable to work outside the home, he took a Saturday job with an engineering firm. But he had also bought himself an extra year in that he would not have to take the dreaded Hebrew exam until the following September 1955.

As the September exam date approached, the couple's second daughter, Becky, was born in August. Ralph's parents paid for someone to care for the girls, and Roberta took up her customary role of assisting Ralph with his studies. Winter worked out his own study program using the century-old but seldom-used *The Englishman's Hebrew Concordance* by Charles Wigram. Roberta and he held their breath as the exam approached. He passed it easily, and then began his second year of Hebrew.

Through preparation for the Hebrew exam, Ralph and Roberta began a book that would make learning Hebrew easier. Roberta and he painstakingly looked up, listed, and defined every word in its order of appearance in the book of Genesis. Then they listed them again in groups of most-to-least used words. Over a year's time, they created what Ralph called *A Contextual Lexicon of Genesis.* The lexicon was designed to save fellow students of Hebrew countless hours referencing a standard dictionary. With the help and prestigious name of Princeton professor Dr. Charles Fritsch attached as coauthor, the *Contextual Lexicon* was presented through a paper written by Winter and delivered by Dr. Fritsch at the annual meeting of the Society of Biblical Literature, and later put into service.

Winter graduated from Princeton Seminary with a Bachelor of Divinity degree in June 1956—the first PhD ever to do so. He wore a doctoral gown from Cornell given to him by his parents. His Princeton graduation was the only one his parents or Ralph attended in his long career of picking up sheepskins. Ralph was right, though, about the usefulness of his accumulated credentials, as he drew on every aspect of his education to arrive at a new paradigm of missionary work in Guatemala.

5

CROSSING THE FRONTIERS

O n June 20, 1956, at the Lamington, New Jersey, church where he had served during his Princeton years, Ralph Winter was ordained in the United Presbyterian Church. Dudley Peck, with whom Winter would soon work as a fellow missionary, gave the commissioning address.

Ralph and Roberta were then off to six months of missionary orientation for an overseas appointment by the Presbyterian Foreign Mission Board (PFMB). This included one month of linguistic training, which the two helped teach, and a month of working with the poor in New York City, where they helped to rebuild damaged buildings and take a census; then four months of lectures, term papers, and logistical details such as writing their wills.

At this time, the Presbyterian Church discouraged mission initiatives that were not started by the denomination itself. Ralph thought this misguided, as he had taken an interest in the religious orders of the Catholic Church. He wrote a term paper on the religious orders as part of his missionary orientation work. These largely self-governed organizations had distinctive strengths, Ralph believed. He saw that Protestant missions had been long delayed until William Carey and Hudson Taylor invented mission agencies with a similar leadership structure to the Catholic orders and likewise a unified governing purpose. His fascination with the Catholic orders would stay with him throughout his life and become a theme in his teaching and the underlying, organizing principle in the umbrella ministry he would one day found.

The Presbyterian Mam Christian Center (MCC), where Dudley and Dorothy Peck had been working with the Mayan Mam Indians for thirty years, was located in the highlands of western Guatemala. It stood in a remote location, about fifteen miles from the nearest paved road and access to public electricity.

Ten years prior to Winter's graduation from Princeton Seminary, the mission board had put in a request for a fraternal worker for the center. They were looking for an ordained minister with training in both linguistics and anthropology, and a spouse who was a registered nurse. Many at the Mam Center thought the position would never be filled due to the unusual requirements, but now it seemed custom-made for Ralph and Roberta. They thought and prayed about accepting the position to which their friend Sam Moffett had alerted them. It certainly met the Trotman criterion that they should do what others could not.

Once committed to the assignment, they hit opposition from the mission board's permanent personnel secretary, who thought that the idea of assigning a PhD to work with an impoverished Indian tribe was a terrible idea. Ralph argued that a people like the Mam, with widespread cultural and spiritual problems, actually needed a PhD working with them. He *could* tear up his PhD diploma, if that would help. The secretary finally relented.

Winter made a visit to the Mam Center prior to his and Roberta's posting there. He still had questions, it seems, as to whether this was the place for them to best serve. At thirty-four years of age, a decade older than most novice missionaries, Ralph knew his character well enough to question whether he would easily adapt to a ministry pattern already established by others. Describing the situation in a letter to his parents, he shows how aware he had become of his need to initiate whenever he saw a problem. The letter's subtext finds him worrying whether this would be wanted by the established authorities. "In one sense," he relates, "the Mam Center is the worst place in the world for us. It is an absolutely fixed pattern that we'll be unable to soon or ever to change. On the other hand it in one small respect is a good place for the very reason it is established. We'll not be forced to decide what to do (and you know how hard that is for me—I've got to study the whole thing down theoretically and through involved analysis decide the path of optimum value, etc.) and won't be blamed—may even be praised—for doing what was done before. This will, more than any other job, perhaps, enable us to follow up other side-line ideas and projects. And that I've got to be able to do or I'll die of ulcers." He ends by saying, "Yet while the inventor's role is partially recognized in the secular world it is not about to be in the ecclesiastical. Too bad." [12]

As it turned out, Ralph and Roberta's assigned task—nurturing indigenous leadership among the Mam, especially pastors—couldn't be done without both "missions engineering" and "cultural engineering." Ralph and Roberta's ways of doing ministry required reinvention, and the Mam had to be introduced to new ways of thinking and acting in order to successfully lead a church community. Ladino pastors were maintaining the church, since the Mam were not accustomed to being accepted as even potential leaders by the Ladino ecclesiastical leadership of the Presbyterian Church. Before arrival, Ralph only understood his compulsion to invent; once in the field, the situation would test Ralph's powers of invention and the flexibility of his superiors.

Conflict with superiors cropped up immediately. After orientation in the States, the Winters were sent to Costa Rica for a year of language school. Winter thought that learning the Mam language was more important than learning the national language, Spanish. The mission had different ideas, believing that the two would need Spanish for basic communication once in Guatemala.

---

12 Letter from Ralph D. Winter to Hugo and Hazel Winter, fall 1957, quoted in Parsons, 2012, 69.

As soon as Spanish instruction began, Winter made the request that Roberta and he be initially assigned to a remote Mam area where they would seldom have to speak Spanish. This request was denied. The health of one of the Winter daughters was cited as the reason, but there was already concern about Ralph's way of doing things.

The methods used at the language school frustrated Winter because of his prior linguistic training. He claimed that he wasn't learning Spanish at all, except in a "really harmful way." What he was learning was "the sight of the words and I find myself having to visualize what I hear or speak in order to understand. This is terrible! Just one carefully designed class (taught by someone besides me) would be a great help—10x as valuable as all we are doing." [13] Winter believed that their school in Costa Rica ought to use the immersion approach adopted by the Army.

In 1961 Robert C. Thorp, the acting secretary for Latin America, heard about Ralph's unhappiness and wrote:

> Their career as missionaries began with their year in Language School in Costa Rica where Dr. Winter could not conform to the pattern of language study as established by the School at the time and consequently did not attend a majority of his classes but rather devised his own system for learning the language at home and spent much time trying to develop a plan for the reorganization of the Language School and its language teaching methods. [14]

Winter's views would eventually be heard. He was later asked by mission leadership to give his suggestions for improving the language school. The impression of someone too smart for his own good lingered, however, among the board's leadership. In fairness,

---

13 Ibid.
14 Letter from Robert C. Thorp to Nathaniel Bercovitz, M.D., February 2, 1961, quoted in Parsons, 2012, 71.

any institution would probably react the same way to a novice threatening revolution, or so it must have seemed. It was a pattern that would be repeated all the way to Lausanne and beyond, leading all the way to a ground-breaking initiative that would be called the Roberta Winter Institute—but we are getting ahead of ourselves.

Guatemala during this period was in a state of political turmoil. The 1950 election of Jacobo Árbenz Guzmán as president turned the country sharply to the left as Guatemala formed a friendly relationship with the Soviet Union. Guzmán's legalization of the Communist party was seen as a threat by the United States, who saw the potential for increased Communist acceptance in Central America.

In 1954 Carlos Castello Armas overthrew the Communist-leaning government, establishing a military dictatorship. The new government was weak, communism remained an underground force, and Armas was assassinated in 1957. Thirty years of guerilla war followed. During this period of unrest, the Presbyterian Church remained well-established in Guatemala, but one can imagine the Winters' fears as they arrived.

The work of Paul and Dora Burgess, who served from 1913 to 1959, and Dudley and Dorothy Peck, who served from 1922 to 1970, laid the foundation for missionary work to the native, non-Latin (Indian) groups in Guatemala. Before this time, almost all missionary work had been directed toward the country's Spanish-speaking population called "Latin" or "Ladinos." The Mayan groups, categorized as "Indians," comprised approximately 60 percent of the Guatemalan population. They were defined as those "living in the old Indian villages, wearing tribal costume, speaking [the Mayan] language and living according to [Mayan] customs." Many of the Spanish-speaking population had some Mayan ancestry themselves.

The Mam were very friendly with the Spanish. Before Spanish occupation of the country, the Mam had been oppressed by the larger Quiché tribe and actually considered the Spanish as liberators. The Mam people, whom the Winters would serve, had assumed Spanish names for this reason. When the Winters arrived in western Guatemala, Dudley and Dorothy Peck were still in the field. At the time, there were some 250,000 Mam in Guatemala, with possibly another 250,000 living in Chiapas, Mexico.

The town nearest the Pecks' mission was San Juan Ostuncalco. With a population of around four thousand, about half of whom were Indian, San Juan had a small Presbyterian church which served fewer than half a dozen families.

Because of the Presbyterians' commitment to working with the Spanish-speaking population, the Pecks had not been assigned to Mam work exclusively during the early years. Working jointly with Mam and Ladinos, they emphasized the unity of their work, urging both groups to worship together. The Mam deferred to the Ladinos on matters within the church and in life in general, which explains the church's emphasis on the Spanish language. Because the tribe's education was limited to only three grades, there were no ordained Mam pastors in Guatemala.

Ralph and Roberta first arrived in the highlands on July 22, 1958. While Paul and Dora Burgess and the Pecks had preceded the Winters—Presbyterian missions in Guatemala dated back to the 1880s—Ralph and Roberta still faced a challenge that qualified as the most extreme form of cross-cultural evangelism in the tripartite division Ralph later used at Lausanne. The Mam had been Westernized to an extent by their Spanish rulers, that was true; but the Mam language bore no relation to any Indo-European language, or any of the ancient languages Ralph and Roberta had studied. The Mam descended from the Mayan civilization and were still wedded to the pantheistic religion of the Maya, in which covenants or pacts were reached with ancestors and deities through ritual sacrifice. The priests or shamans of the native religion remained authorities in the villages. The Mam were very much a distinct people, both from the mainstream Ladinos of Guatemalan culture and other tribes such as the Quiché.

The Mam's tendency to be submissive both to the Quiché and the Ladinos did not mean that they could be easily drawn into worshiping with them. It meant that the few who attended these churches kept quiet, while the vast majority had no interest, preferring the Mayan religion they considered their own. In 1958 only about two hundred Mam could be counted as Presbyterians. With the relative neglect of the Presbyterian mission and the ill-considered policy of integrated worship, much work remained to be done.

Ralph and Roberta quickly began observing the cultural patterns among the Mam people. Ralph's anthropological and engineering background led him to try to absorb all he could about Mam cultural issues, including the role of the priest or shaman in Mam society, native problems with alcoholism, and the behavioral assumptions about engagement and marriage. Dudley Peck observed:

> They questioned us about every phase of the work. Their keen analysis of the local situation and anthropologically-oriented understanding of the cultural differences between the Indian and the Ladino neighbors has contributed to their finding themselves as members of the community. It has been a delightful and stimulating experience to rethink with them the community-service approach in winning the Mam-speaking people to faith in Christ as Savior and Lord. [15]

Roberta described her experience a year after their arrival, saying:

---

15 Dudley H. Peck, report of the Guatemala Mission's annual meeting (1959), 1, quoted in Parsons, 2012, 81.

It has also been a year of getting acquainted—of visiting in Indian homes, of attendance at Indian births and
harvest "cultos" (festivals), of learning to know well the
leaders in the Mam Center. We have taken part in the
weekly services, the graduation program of the Institute,
and the Christmas gatherings in all the surrounding
communities. In all this we have learned much about the
culture as well as listening constantly to spoken Mam.
More and more we feel an accepted part of the Mam
Christian community … I am looking forward to the
day when we will really be one with the people. [16]

Unity with the people would not come easily or quickly. Ralph
would later be criticized in mission circles for his emphasis on cross-
cultural evangelism by commentators who, at times, were under
the impression that Ralph did not realize the difficulties involved.
In Guatemala, Winter's assignment was to develop leaders and
pastors and to grow a truly indigenous Mam church. In doing so
Ralph came to understand all too well how much more easily Mam
leadership might reach other members of their tribe. Neighbor-
to-neighbor evangelism was always more effective, but the fire of
God's love had to be kindled in enough hearts to take hold.

Ralph faced four major problems in his efforts to nurture an
indigenous Mam church. The first problem was the Mam language
itself. Dudley and Dorothy Peck began studying the language as
soon as they arrived in the country. By 1927, after five years, they
produced a draft of the New Testament in the Mam language.
The translation was wooden, studiously literal, and little used.
Dorothy also developed a rough primer in order to teach the
Mam how to write. No other written documents besides the
New Testament and the primer existed in the Mam language.

16   Roberta Winter, report of the Guatemala Mission's annual meeting (1959), 1–2,
quoted in Parsons, 2012, 81.

Learning the Mam language, while a priority for the Winters and their Presbyterian mission board, proved to be extremely difficult for Ralph, given the fact that the Winters were required to first learn Spanish. Dorothy Peck did not volunteer to teach the language to the Winters, and she was the only Westerner to speak it well and understand its structure. Perhaps Ralph's credentials in linguistics made her think—at least, initially—that the effort would be unnecessary. Most of the younger Mam men were reluctant to use their own language, preferring to speak Spanish in order to fit in with the larger society. There were fewer occasions than one might suppose when use of the Mam language was essential. On the other hand, the use of another's mother tongue constitutes the most powerful bridge across cultural divides, as Ralph well knew.

Ralph's answer to learning this difficult language was typically innovative. He had, among the group of young men he was mentoring at the time, a Mam tribesman named Ruben Dias. Like most Mam, Ruben had only a third-grade education, but he proved to have a brilliant mind. Ralph's idea was to devise a number of skits portraying everyday Mam life, which he would have Dias write out in the Mam language. By observing the recognizable activities while memorizing the skits, Winter thought he could acquire a beginning level of proficiency and advance from there.

He introduced Dias to the typewriter and was astonished at how fast the young man mastered it. Then he introduced Dias to the concept of developing the skits, and the purpose for them, expressing that they should not only impart language information but also give him and Roberta a feel for village life and the people's customs and mores.

He imagined that it would take several days for Dias to produce a few skits, and was amazed when Dias returned three skits to him, finished, by the end of the first day, along with a translation of the Lord's Prayer and a list of church terms.

While learning the Mam language was a priority, Winter could not devote full time to it. His other missionary duties included administering a Bible school, overseeing a school that taught basic Spanish to Mam children, and helping out with any problems related to the facilities. In addition, he was expected to take an active role in village life in order to gain acceptance. All this while being required by the Presbyterian mission board to learn a difficult tribal language. The Winters were asked to present proof of progress in language acquisition by the end of their first year. Ralph kept thinking, "If we had only been allowed to learn Mam first!"

Sadly, Winter never really mastered the Mam language. This caused him continual trouble with the mission board. When asked in 1959 about his progress with learning Mam, Winter outlined his previous twenty-one weeks of service in Guatemala, noting that only nine and one-half of these weeks had been available "for anything like language learning." What he did not divulge was the amount of time he had devoted to his own ideas about how to serve the Mam.

Recalling the Winters' delays in learning Mam, Robert Thorp noted that Winter "apparently was involving himself in too many other activities and was not learning the language. At least he was not apparently following the usual patterns of learning a language, but rather dabbling in new methods and techniques which he himself had devised." Thorp viewed Winter's "fertile imagination" the way so many others would, as ingenious but irritating. His continuing comments indulge in armchair psychology:

> Dr. Winter is undoubtedly bothered by the fact that at the age of 36 he still has not found his niche. He rationalizes his failure to learn the Mam language on the basis that he is basically an engineer or that he might not stay on at the Mam Center or that he has too many other responsibilities. [17]

Thorp sums up the case by depicting Ralph as at odds with his own powers, and this finally provokes in Thorp a measure of sympathy:

> A great deal could be written about his transient ideas and schemes, many of them impracticable and not founded upon careful planning. Others of them are actually brilliant. (Most of them are not taken seriously by his fellow workers, which must increase his frustrations.) He is almost a genius, with a versatile, productive mind, and his time and activity cannot keep pace with it. [18]

Thorp's portrait of Ralph at thirty-six has its truth. Although Ralph would be much more effective in the years immediately following than Thorp could have imagined, I don't doubt that Ralph's long education in harnessing his abilities caused him anguish. That's a staple among creative people.

Others were even less kind than Thorp, finding Winter's way of doing things impractical or burdensome. Roberta reported one missionary as saying that it didn't matter what was suggested. If Winter was involved, they would be automatically against it.

Upon returning to Guatemala after his and Roberta's 1962 furlough at the end of their first five-year term, Ralph was practically commanded by mission leadership to focus on learning Mam. A letter from mission board executive John H. Sinclair to Winter attached the motions of the joint committee (Guatemala) and noted:

> I know that there will be many demands upon you immediately upon your arrival to get into other activities, but I trust you will have the good judgment and the grace to put aside all other tasks, perhaps even some needful

---

17 Letter from Robert C. Thorp to Nathaniel Bercovitz, February 2, 1961, quoted in Parsons, 2012, 85.
18 Ibid.

projects that challenge your fertile imagination, and give yourselves to the task of learning well the language. [19]

Despite the difficult Mam language, Ralph remained undeterred in his mission of forming Mam leadership. That so many Mam also spoke Spanish certainly helped.

The Mam's abject poverty posed a second major problem, however. In order to communicate the reality of a loving God, the Winters felt they needed to provide practical solutions to the people's economic struggles. Roberta describes their impoverished state:

> They were—and are—very poor, probably the most impoverished group of their size in the entire hemisphere. Thus, missionary outreach to them had to combine not only evangelism and church planting, but also agricultural, medical and economic and educational work.

> Their one-room huts were made of mud with dirt floors and three stones strategically placed in the middle of the floor to serve as a fireplace-stove. Their clothes (of which they had only one change) were patched and re-patched; in fact where the women carried their babies on their back, the patch itself was very often patched. The Mam diet was almost completely corn, with a bit of black beans once a week perhaps, and a tiny bit of meat for a very special and somewhat rare occasion. They had no milk, no eggs, no other vegetables or fruits—there was just no money for these. They raised chickens [for sale], but could not afford to eat either their eggs or the chickens themselves. [20]

---

19 Letter from John H. Sinclair to Ralph and Roberta Winter, July 10, 1961, 1, quoted in Parsons, 2012, 84.
20 Roberta H. Winter, 2000, 20, quoted in Parsons, 2012, 81.

The poverty of the Mam people was largely the result of a subsistence-farming culture, in which family plots were broken down steadily as fathers passed on land to multiple sons. The land was mountainous (western Guatemala lies at approximately ten thousand feet) and the people widely dispersed. The cost of one tortilla was about a penny, and a man's average salary was less than forty cents a day.

While Winter's job was to create church leaders among the Mam, the tribe was too poor to support pastors once they were developed. Mam men were tied to the land they cultivated through inheritance and so could not be expected to relocate to pastor widespread churches. Roberta Winter describes her and Ralph's work with the Mam as directed by their understanding of the crushing poverty of this outcast people. She states, "Something had to be done to help them economically even if to support their churches was the only reason to climb out of extreme poverty ... There was simply no way to ignore the distressing economic problem which influenced everything in their lives—certainly any future in leadership development." [21]

In order to minister to their material needs, the Winters were to have to scratch for resources, because the Guatemala Mission itself tended to direct its resources toward the Spanish-speaking population. During the two five-year terms the Winters worked at the Mam Center, Presbyterian missionaries working with the Ladinos in the capital city visited them only once. They were shocked at the poverty they saw.

Ralph could only nurture an indigenous Mam church, he concluded, if he helped create a sustainable local economy. Such an economy would need to be designed with two purposes: (1) the general welfare of the population, and (2) the rise within it of particular businesses and trades that allowed potential pastors of a future Mam church to be self-supporting. Most pastors in Latin

---

21 Winter, "Winter Initiatives," 22.

America, even among the Spanish-speaking population, were bivocational, and so must be these far-poorer Indian pastors.

Ralph had few resources with which to accomplish this economic transformation of Mam society. Money from the New York offices went first to the mission's office in Guatemala City, where the funds were delegated for various projects. Winter's annual budget was a paltry $650.

In addition to his allocated budget, Winter's friends in the United States sent him money designated for his work. Winter carefully put these funds into a special bank account, never mixing it with personal funds.

He then used this money to set up several small businesses, teaching the young men he was training for the ministry how to do the work required and to administer the businesses themselves. He eventually started fourteen of these businesses.

Wherever possible, the businesses started by Winter were portable in nature, so that prospective pastors could benefit from them wherever they were appointed to serve. Among these were a photography business with a residential photo lab, several foot-loom weaving businesses, and a print shop. He even started a business that provided basic dentistry, mostly pulling rotten teeth. Several of the men were taught to drive a jeep (purchased by the Winters for $300), and they eventually ran the first ambulance service for the mission clinic.

The one exception to the portability rule was a furniture-making project called Industrias Tecnicas (Technical Industries). This rural factory made folding chairs and church pews, and later closets and doors for a housing development in Quetzaltenango, a mostly Indian city and Guatemala's second largest. Industrias Tecnicas was run by the inimitable Ruben Dias.

Winter felt strongly that cultural progress among the Mam people had to be securely based on their knowing how to keep track of money. He had recently learned how to do this himself through a self-education project that reminds one of how he learned to play chords on the piano. Being required to keep the books for the Mam Center, Winter decided to learn accounting. With no prior experience, he bought a 500-page standard text and for three months spent every evening from 7 p.m. until midnight studying. He learned the discipline so well that he became the accounting expert for the entire Guatemala mission effort. (In everything he would do for years to come, he kept an eagle eye on the books and often found errors others missed. He was a visionary and a number cruncher at the same time.)

So he stressed the importance of accounting with those who were given the businesses to run, teaching them double-entry bookkeeping as well as operations. Strict accounting was particularly important for the Mam, because the Ladino population routinely tried to cheat them.

In the case of Industrias Tecnicas, which handled thousands of dollars each month, not only Dias but the five young men working under him all learned bookkeeping and accounting. Winter also stressed the idea of saving profits and reinvesting them in the business. In order to set an example of thrift, the Winters refused to drink colas, knowing that their purchase would set a bad example. The men in Mam society often denied food to their families in order to buy alcohol and luxuries.

Weaving operations were set up for the Mam women. There was a government school that taught them to manufacture textiles, and the Winters taught them to market and distribute the finished goods. The idea was to allow the women to make enough money to buy milled corn, freeing them from having to grind their own. The women's businesses were profitable and would have been successful had not their husbands taken the money from them as soon as it came into their hands. As an internal report later stated, "The idea was not a bad one; it just didn't take into consideration the cultural factors of the husbands toward their wives."

As a whole the businesses begun and administered by the Winters went far as an aid to church planting and facilitating rural pastorships.

The problem of authority, as it related to the Mam and the missionaries themselves, posed a third major challenge. There was a severe relational issue among the missionaries at the Mam Center. The personality conflicts, as difficult as they were, were not as much the real problem as an impediment to solving that problem.

The shamans of the Mayan religion held such authority within Mam society because they were prepared to deal with spiritual and physical issues alike. The allocation of the two issues to different professionals—ministers and medical personnel—did not make sense to the Mam.

Winter observed that missionaries who performed only medical work were not highly regarded by the people, because they did not teach or preach; pastors were held in low regard if they did not also do medical work. Ralph wanted to integrate the two functions as much as possible. He believed that the church's work would be enhanced if its pastors were trained in basic medical work and its medical workers trained in spiritual counseling. In fact, he thought that with basic medical training pastors might handle 90 percent of the cases they would see.

He later explained the differences between the Western view of medicine and the Mam view with an illustration. A Mam couple waits in line at a medical clinic. Asked their problem, they reply, "It's our daughter." When asked why they had not brought their daughter in, they say, "She's not sick." Then asked why they are there, they reply, "The problem is whether she should marry this certain person."

If they consulted a shaman, he would think the matter over with them, consult his pouch of medicines, perform a ceremony, and make a decision that satisfied the couple.

Western medical personnel would simply kick the couple out of the clinic. The failure of Christian medical workers to perform the role of shaman through Christian counseling led the people to return to their Mayan priests for their spiritual needs. The Mam had no concept of specialization within their culture, whereas the missionaries from the U.S. insisted upon it.

One medical missionary in particular insisted upon it—Ruth Wardell—the nurse who ran the Mam Center Clinic.

Ruth arrived in 1949 to run the clinic the Pecks had started. She was a faithful, committed missionary, who lived serving the Mam for many years. She was also a perfectionist with a "high-powered" personality. She had set ways of doing things and was not open to others' opinions. She controlled the clinic with an iron fist and refused to allow either the other missionaries or the Indians to participate in the work there, except for the two Mam who gave out the medicine and administered the shots she ordered. While Roberta was a trained nurse who had finished at the top of her class at USC, Ruth would not let her work in the clinic unless Ruth was present.

Ruth believed that medically trained missionaries should decide what medical work should include; Winter wanted to see an effective connection between medical work and evangelism. And he simply wanted to multiply the number of people who could solve common medical problems. This created enormous tension, as Ruth saw the issue purely as an infringement on her authority to run the clinic as she liked. The Winters soon realized that the relationship with Ruth did not even remotely approach what could be considered a workable one.

The Ruth Wardell situation was oppressive to the Winters, especially Ralph, who was always trying to engineer solutions to problems.

Remarkably, Ralph maintained an equable attitude toward Ruth. Their differences never resulted in harsh words on Ralph's part. A 1961 letter from Robert Thorp notes that Winter "is considerate of others and would prefer a transfer to another field rather than staying on there if that meant being influential in a nurse being removed from that work to which she came earlier than he." [22]

---

22 Letter from Robert C. Thorp to Nathaniel Bercovitz, M.D., February 2, 1961, 2, quoted in Parsons, 2012, 307.

Trouble between Ruth Wardell and the mission leadership culminated in a contentious meeting of the Mam Center staff where proposals for future work integration were discussed. There is evidence that Ruth managed to delay the meeting for months. Winter described it to Sinclair: "It came up about what Roberta should do when Ruth is absent (for a week or weekend). She [Ruth] said that inasmuch as she is the director of medical work, when she goes, the clinic is closed." When asked what should happen if an emergency case was brought to Roberta at such a time, Ruth replied that those cases should be taken to hospitals in Quetzaltenango. When Roberta remarked that this would make her look ill-trained or heartless in the eyes of the people, Ruth said under her breath, but distinctly, "One of the two of us will have to leave."[23]

Shortly thereafter, following a rebuke, "she [Ruth] stood up and left with these words: 'You now have a new director for the clinic, and you have my resignation—this is very official.' Everyone felt very bad. No further discussion with her was possible."[24]

Her resignation did not stick. While the clinic was run under a different board as of January 1963, it continued to operate the way Ruth wanted it to until her retirement in 1980.

There's evidence, however, that Ralph went around Ruth Wardell, integrating medicine and evangelism—very likely with Roberta at his side. The American Hospital in Guatemala City, a Presbyterian institution, had broadened its outreach to the people through its own school of nursing. It believed in combining medical work and evangelism, too. A 1959 field report from the hospital states that, because the Mam Center had adopted their integrated approach, its medical work had "been especially successful in reaching the needs of the Mam people and in combating the domination of the witch doctors who combine religion, healing and a lot of psychology (of a kind) for their own purpose."

---

23 Letters from Ralph D. Winter to John Sinclair, February 28 and March 13–14, 1962, quoted in Parsons, 2012, 308.
24 Ibid.

Meeting these other challenges prepared the way for nurturing Christian leaders among the Mam and building church communities. The task demanded both spiritual formation and education far beyond the three primary grades supplied to the Mam by Guatemala's public schools.

Almost from the beginning of his field service in Guatemala, Winter began mentoring young men as he had first learned to do through the Navigators' discipleship programs. He taught Bible classes at first in a classroom setting, the way the other missionaries did, but soon realized a more personal approach would be better. He started holding meetings in his living room. There he had his group of Mam men study Bible passages with the goal of discovering how these could be applied to their lives. The method led the men to understand the passages more clearly, as well as to think of ways to apply the Word to everyday living.

As Winter worked with his group, he came to realize that his assigned students were not from the Mam mainstream. They were, for one reason or another, social outcasts, orphans or people struggling with alcoholism, who would have a hard time being accepted as authorities by the broader Mam community. Winter wondered how he could reach the natural leaders of the Mam, and if he did, how he could provide the education they would need to become pastors.

At least a sixth-grade education was required before seminary training could begin—three more grades than the rural schools provided.

Winter learned that anyone over the age of fourteen with three years of education could receive a diploma for a complete, six-year elementary education by passing a state-administered test. In fact, the government had devised a series of tests that could be passed for even higher certifications as a way of addressing the needs of students who became sick just before graduation.

If Ralph could devise a curriculum that could be delivered to the Mam or others who needed it where they lived, then he might attract natural leaders and encourage them to consider becoming pastors. Anyone who wanted the advantage of a sixth-grade education could participate. He would have something of practical benefit to offer the whole community.

Ralph went to work devising a correspondence/extension system that included students meeting with teachers at scheduled intervals.

Winter then sought government authorization for his adult distance-education program. While at the Mam Center, he had previously started two schools: the Inter-American School, where his daughters and the children of other missionaries received their elementary school education, and a junior high called the Colegio Lincoln, used by the local town's leaders and the Ladino population. This gave him the necessary standing to receive government authorization for the adult distance-education program.

Taking time for education still remained a problem. No Mam adult could be expected to attend an additional three years of school, even through correspondence courses. Was there a way of minimizing "school work"—traditional written assignments—and still imparting the skills necessary to pass the state-administered test? A more innovative approach to the curriculum was needed than Ralph initially thought.

With the help of Jim Emery, a Presbyterian missionary who worked in the coastal regions, and the support of several other mission organizations, Winter devised a series of "vertical" textbooks, each covering a different subject through several years of study. A student could work his way up to the required level of proficiency from any starting point beyond third grade, with tutoring provided only as needed. The textbooks emphasized a question-and-answer approach that led to mastery of the subject matter rather than the time-consuming written assignments typical of correspondence courses.

When the Winters took the new textbooks to the minister of education of Guatemala, he was, according to Roberta, "a bit surprised, hesitated, and said, 'But we have just now published an entirely new curriculum from the first through the sixth grade.' But [Ralph] had already gotten wind of this and we had followed the new curriculum even before it was published." The minister was relieved and pleased.

Winter did not see the new educational delivery system as merely a way around an obstacle or an evangelistic incentive. He thought it had real educational advantages, because it appealed to the self-motivated person who was a natural leader. The men it would attract would be following an important biblical and historic path. He said:

> I believe it to be sound in the fullest biblical and Presbyterian sense for men to be ordained by [the] Presbytery who have not been called to a professional ministry. The fact that the Apostle Paul and in fact most Presbyterian ministers in history up until recent times have had a hand in agriculture (or other) along with their congregation is not to be sniffed at. I fully believe in a professional ministry, but not to the exclusion of other men ministering. [25]

With the certification received by taking Winter's adult education course and passing the required exam, Mam men could then go to seminary, receive a degree, and so become ordained.

By 1962 a number of Presbyterian missionaries were focused on training national pastors. To facilitate this, the main Presbyterian seminary was moved from Guatemala City to a location closer to most of the Presbyterian churches, which were in the western part of the country. While this was helpful, it did not do much

---

[25] Letter from Ralph D. Winter to John H. Sinclair, February 4, 1963, quoted in Parsons, 2012, 100.

for those in rural areas, nor for busy church elders who could not attend school weekly because of their heavy responsibilities.

Winter and Jim Emery undertook a study to see how training was conducted in other Latin American countries. They discovered that in Brazil there were a large number of ordained clergy who were also lay professionals. This confirmed their mutual conviction that beginning indigenous churches with a bivocational clergy made sense.

All that was needed was the development of an entirely new and transferable system of theological education.

6

SOLVING AN EQUATION
OF DISTANCE AND TIME

By 1962 Ralph Winter had become a member of the seminary board and Jim Emery the institution's head. Emery and Winter began to consider a radical solution to the problem of providing enough seminary education to the natural leaders of local church communities for them to be ordained. Without this, a truly indigenous church in Guatemala would never grow—one had hardly been started among the Mam. No one from among its quarter million in population had ever graduated from the Presbyterian seminary—no one had even attended.

The performance of the Presbyterian Seminary of Guatemala had been dismal. Begun in 1938, only ten of the more than two hundred students trained there were still functioning as pastors. Most of the institution's graduates never entered the ministry at all, or left it for other occupations. Students brought there from rural areas became accustomed to urban life and never returned to the economically depressed villages they had been expected to serve.

As with the sixth-grade diploma program, Winter and Emery starting thinking about training the natural leaders of church in those communities. How would they go about this? And from where would the money come? By virtue of Emery's position as seminary head and Ralph's on its board, they knew that they could not keep the traditional seminary going and launch a new venture in extension education. They would have to propose shutting down

the conventional seminary for what came to be known initially
as the "Guatemala Experiment." Board approval would require a
supreme effort of planning and advocacy.

Education by extension was not a brand new concept. As early
as 1951, the Southern Baptist Convention (SBC) had begun educating pastors with the first Christian extension program—one that
led to a college diploma for its graduates. The idea was to produce
pastors with both college and seminary educations, and by 1960
the program had over three thousand enrollees. The University
of South Africa's extension program dated to the 1940s, and the
University of London had recently started its Open University
for students who, due to time and monetary restraints, could not
attend traditional classes. These programs operated primarily
through correspondence courses. They were proving ideal for older
students with family and job commitments, as well as for students
who lacked the necessary prior education for university acceptance.

Winter was a great innovator, but he also knew from his
anthropological studies that 90 percent of all innovation in human
society is copied from somewhere else. He was smart enough
to learn as much as possible from what had already been done.
What Winter and Emery finally devised as a solution to educating Guatemala's future Presbyterian clergy proved far more novel,
however, than anything to date.

For one thing, the student body changed from young people to
the recognized lay leaders of the church communities. These men
were enlisted in a fashion more like the military than application
to a university.

They were also enrolled at whatever level of academic achievement beyond third grade they happened to possess. As with
Winter and Emery's sixth-grade vertical curriculum, the new
studies they designed allowed students to begin with sixth-grade,
ninth-grade, twelfth-grade, and two-year college educations.
The student could make himself eligible for a seminary degree
from anywhere along that continuum.

The first iteration of their curriculum did not work as well as they hoped. The take-home studies didn't "take" because the men could not effectively handle assignments from traditional textbooks on a home-study basis. Winter and Emery then rewrote the curriculum in a form designed specifically for home study.

In Guatemala, interaction between teachers and students could neither be facilitated by a centralized location nor by correspondence. The students required personal instruction but in locations that were within walking distance. A network of "extension centers" was set up all over the country where missionaries and others working in those areas could provide three hours of tutoring once a week. In addition, all students were required to attend two-day meetings each month at the main campus of the seminary. Because of its relatively small size, this was possible in Guatemala. Bus transport was widely available and cheap.

The final innovation of the "Guatemala Experiment" was its reliance on government exams for certification. Ralph again made use of laws designed to enable Guatemalans to complete their studies through examinations in the case of sickness. The students who went through Winter and Emery's program were able, in this way, to complete officially recognized degrees. Ralph always thought it a mistake for seminaries to give degrees, like the MDiv or ThD, that were peculiar to theological education. He believed in following the Bachelor's, Master's, and PhD pattern common throughout the global university system. Commonly recognized degrees were much better badges of expertise and passports to working in different cultures.

The campaign to suspend normal operations at the seminary and try the Guatemala Experiment began with Emery's credibility as leader of the institution. Both Winter and Emery emphasized they wanted to do this through the seminary, not apart from it. Emery had influence on the staff, and Winter, because of his PhD, had influence with the board. Between the two men, the program gained approval, at least technically.

During the 1963–64 school year, the normal operations at the seminary were suspended in favor of Winter and Emery's new program. TEE (Theological Education by Extension) was born.

In 1964 the program appeared to be succeeding until a required meeting was attended by only twenty students. A devastating rain and lack of promotion were the likely causes. Also, the program produced no graduates that year, which was disappointing.

The mission board considered rescinding its approval of the program and returning to conventional seminary operations. Winter and Emery fought to postpone reopening the seminary for at least one year. That way, they would be able to "work one more year with the one hundred men in the extension wing, [and] find out which of them are really worth it." Winter argued that most of the older missionaries would be out of the work in Guatemala within a few years, and they might as well see forty good men established in ministry in the region.

At first, TEE received little support among the local, traditionally trained pastors in Guatemala. These men had spent years in established seminaries and would not believe that an equal education could be obtained without years of residential training. That was, of course, the settled practice in the U.S., and the Guatemalans wanted nothing less. As Emery and Winter worked to change the thinking within the seminary board, Ralph wrote

> We can still hope that some of the nationals will catch a vision of the extension approach to the problem. But as long as we, in the U.S., go on for all practical purposes ignoring the biblical and theological possibility of men in their 30s going into the ministry, we ought not to feel very greatly abused by events here if the U.S. example speaks louder than we can here in the board meetings! [26]

---

[26] Letter from Ralph D. Winter to Jim Emery and Chuck Ainley, June 11, 1964, quoted in Parsons, 2012, 112.

Years later, Winter explained that a lack of ordained pastors was one reason that TEE was kept alive that year and so ultimately succeeded:

> Presbyterians have representatives who are both elders and pastors, but if the church doesn't have an ordained pastor, one elder will come from that church. (Normally, a pastor and an elder come to the meeting.) So there were maybe 60 or 70 churches, but there were no ordained pastors yet ... [these elders] came and they outvoted all of those capital [city] pastors and sustained the program. [27]

One more year was all it took for the program to take off. With the same funds available, the student body soon increased from the seven who attended the conventional seminary to two hundred taught by three full-time and twelve part-time faculty members.

The program began having its effect in the Guatemalan Presbyterian community as a whole. Ross Kinsler, who became the third leader of TEE, made note of a gathering that reflected sudden, phenomenal growth in the Presbyterian community. [28] A congregation of between twelve hundred and two thousand gathered at one church with a seminary choir of thirty-five. Nothing like this had ever been seen in Guatemala before.

Within a short time, most of the pastors in the Guatemalan Presbyterian Church, as well as in many other denominations, would come out of the TEE program. As Roberta Winter observed, these men "have proven themselves equal to any seminary-trained pastor in the country." She and others also noted that, because extension-trained pastors could be involved daily with the people while they were training for ordination, they were usually

---

27 Interview with Ralph Winter by Greg Parsons on August 16, 2006, quoted in Parsons, 2012, 114.
28 Parsons, 2012, 116.

more useful than pastors who were full-time students and not
involved in day-to-day work during their educations.

Not only was TEE a success in Guatemala, it rapidly became a
model for developing church leaders among the formerly hidden
peoples (unreached peoples) served by Christian missions around
the globe.

In 1965, Winter was elected to be the executive secretary of
the Association of Latin American Theological Schools, Northern
Region, an organization he had helped to found. He used this
position to travel throughout Latin America promoting TEE
to wide acceptance.

In 1966, Winter began a series of articles for *World Vision
Magazine*. In the first article, he described some of the thinking
behind TEE. By the time the article was written, TEE had already
been adopted by the California Friends Mission in Guatemala
and Honduras. They had thirteen regional centers educating
eighty-five students.

A meeting in Colombia in September 1967 brought together
parties from across Latin America who had shown an interest
in TEE. This meeting began the worldwide spread of TEE in
earnest. By mid-1969, Winter would write that TEE "has become
the catalyst of a whole movement involving more than 50 other
schools in Latin America, and there is serious interest around the
world."[29] In that same article, Winter told of men being trained,
or having already been trained, in Bolivia and Colombia as well
as in Guatemala.

In 1971, Winter and another enthusiastic supporter of TEE,
Ralph Covell, traveled the globe spreading the word of how to
educate an indigenous clergy in the worst circumstances.
They went from France to Pakistan, then on to Thailand, the
Philippines, Hong Kong, and Japan. Winter met with at least

---

29 Ralph D. Winter, "The Seminary That Became a Movement," *World Vision Magazine*
(1969: Monrovia World Vision, Inc. 13:10), 8, quoted in Parsons, 2012, 114.

587 seminary leaders on that trip, adding their names to the mailing list of *Extension,* a newsletter devoted to the program.

For two decades and more, TEE became a crucial new model for seminary education around the world. There is still a huge TEE program in India. TEE gave cross-cultural missionaries a means of nurturing an indigenous clergy in situations where that seemed impossible.

It also raised Ralph Winter's profile and opened up new opportunities for what he started to call "missions engineering."

7

LESSONS LEARNED AND TAUGHT

I n 1966 the Winters returned to the United States on their second furlough from Guatemala. They believed they would be returning at the end of the year, although they had not forgotten their conflicts with the mission board. Still, they left all of their belongings behind as they had done for their first furlough five years earlier. Ralph's heart was now firmly fixed on his work with TEE and expanding church leadership by ordaining indigenous leaders through extension education. While he had misgivings about his effectiveness there, and despite the conflicts of purpose and personality already outlined, he had no intention of leaving unless asked.

Back in Pasadena, Winter's work with TEE, as well as some of his writing on mission structure in general, had captured the attention of Donald McGavran, who was just starting the School of World Mission (SWM) at Fuller Theological Seminary. [30] McGavran and Alan Tippett began running this specialized graduate school program to serve furloughed missionaries in 1965. Their student body was made up exclusively of missionaries from various denominations, all of whom had at least three years of field experience and were planning on returning to overseas positions. McGavran and Tippet were SWM's only two faculty members in the beginning.

---

30 The School of World Mission is now called the School of Intercultural Studies. It remains a vital part of Fuller Theological Seminary.

Charles Fuller, the seminary's founder, knew Winter through Ralph's friendship with his son Dan. He was getting to know him now in a deeper and more appreciative way through his writings. Winter, impressed by McGavran's 1955 book, *The Bridges of God,* sent McGavran an article he had written, "Gimmickitis." The article was one of a series he had written on what he called the "Seven Deadly Missionary Sins." In "Gimmickitis," Winter outlined a list of worthwhile things that became ends in themselves and detracted from the essential work of establishing and growing churches.

McGavran was impressed by Winter's thinking and had the article published in the *Church Growth Bulletin* in 1966.

When Winter contacted McGavran on his return to Pasadena for his furlough, McGavran made Ralph an offer to join Tippett and him as a faculty member at the School of World Mission.

Winter liked the idea of working a professorship at SWM into his mission work, and proposed that he teach alternating semesters, returning to Guatemala every other six months. McGavran agreed with this plan, and Winter excitedly accepted the offer.

After McGavran suffered health problems that year, coming close to death on two occasions, he decided that Winter was needed on a full-time basis and told him this was the only way the agreement could work.

Two things were at play in Ralph Winter's world at this time. One was the dedication of ten years' work in the Guatemala highlands and the expansion of TEE from his position there. The other was his "big picture" view of his role in God's kingdom. He saw that a faculty position at Fuller Seminary would provide him with outstanding colleagues and put him in a place where he could have influence on church growth and missions worldwide. There were also practical considerations. On the field he had no access to a secretary or assistant—other than Roberta—to help him organize his ideas and produce necessary correspondence. An office and secretary and a secure position as a seminary professor would give him the structure he needed to develop and disseminate his ideas.

Behind these reasons lay Winter's frustrations. In his 1965 personal report, Winter reflected on his talents and their larger purposes. He writes:

> My life revolves around planning and scheming. My forte is less that of following through doggedly in routine details ... Books flow endlessly into this house and ideas pour ceaselessly out of my heart and life ... If I suffer, then, it is because I cannot, even at 41–42, depend on assistants ... to help me fulfill what knowledge and experience lead me legitimately to expect to be able to do. [31]

Although initially shocked by McGavran's change in their agreement, Winter saw the wisdom of accepting the position as a full-time assignment. After the first semester was over, Roberta and he returned to Guatemala to retrieve their belongings in preparation for Ralph's new career. Because of the protracted guerilla warfare engulfing the country, the Winters would not return to the Mam in Guatemala again for over thirty-five years. They did, however, visit Guatemala City twice in the intervening years.

Winter became the School of World Mission's third faculty member. The Presbyterian mission board, not wanting to lose the Winters after all, agreed to "loan" Winter to Fuller and the SWM while continuing his mission support for five years. Fuller insisted on paying the board what they would have paid him as a faculty member. Winter served at Fuller Seminary for the next ten years, teaching some one thousand missionaries.

Winter's colleague Donald McGavran was a major influence in what was becoming known as the "Church Growth Movement." Born in India, the son and grandson of missionaries, McGavran followed his parents as a missionary to his birthplace. He saw

---

31 Personal Report Outline (half filled out in 1964 for 1963, then completed in 1965, signed September 17, 1965), 4, quoted in Parsons, 2012, 149.

flaws in the way churches were trying to grow in traditionally
non-Christian countries. Where churches were trying to convert
individuals, growth was slow. It became McGavran's belief that
people did not want to be converted individually by outsiders;
if they were to convert at all, it was more likely that they would
do so in groups, with others like themselves. This was the way
Europe had been Christianized. Why should the rest of the
world be different? Even if mass conversion meant that many
were initially converted with only a rudimentary understanding
of their new allegiance to Christianity, such mass conversions
resulted in good long-term results historically among many people
groups, from the tribes of Northern Europe to South India. Slow
individual conversions, on the other hand, had historically made
little impact on people groups with high levels of cohesiveness,
because any convert was immediately ostracized. People would
find comfort in worshiping God within their own cultural patterns, and the church would grow. As the Bible was translated and
the people learned to read and study it, families and individuals
would find the personal relationship with Christ that would begin
to transform their lives. The concept came to be known as the
"Homogeneous Unit Principle," or HUP.

McGavran was hugely influenced by Methodist bishop J.
Wascom Pickett, who had succeeded in converting large numbers
of people through what he called "mass movements to Christ."
(Because he thought the phrase might be associated with mass
evangelism crusades, McGavran would refer to "people movements to Christ" or "Christward movements.") Pickett's ideas were
revolutionary and effective, but might have died in 1930s' India
except for Donald McGavran, who said of Pickett, "He kindled
my concern that the Church grow. I lit my candle at Pickett's
fire." [32] It would be another twenty years before McGavran would

---

32 D. A. McGavran and G. G. Hunter, *Church Growth: Strategies that Work*
(Nashville: Abingdon, 1980), 14, quoted in Parsons, 2012, 162.

write The Bridges of God, which spread Pickett's ideas to a point where, according to Pickett's biographer, Arthur G. McPhee, "the missiological world could no longer ignore them." [33]

While the church growth concept received a lot of criticism, as many believed that it sought only to increase church membership rolls or to create cultural Christians at the expense of delivering the real message of salvation, McGavran saw its greater wisdom historically. Drawing on his experiences in India and his travels to other countries, he was convinced that faith had to follow cultural lines, at least where these did not oppose Christianity directly. Winter saw McGavran as a man who "had a practical sense of what's important and what isn't important" and recognized that he "didn't jive with anybody's traditional thinking at all," [34] an attribute Winter applauded.

While McGavran took the activist role at SWM, Tippett was the scholar and academic. He provided analysis to bolster McGavran's and, later, Winter's ideas.

Teaching was never Winter's primary interest, but it was his primary assignment at Fuller. Specifically, he was to teach TEE and statistics. As missionaries, McGavran and Tippett—like Winter—saw teaching as secondary to developing ideas and initiatives that would spread God's word to the unreached. The three wanted to direct the knowledge of their experienced students into more effective mission strategies. As Roberta Winter wrote later, her husband's "main concern (and his gifting) was discovering the missing links in what is necessary for missionary advance and then working to produce what is necessary to fill that need." [35] Winter called himself a "scholar activist."

Later Winter would take on the task of teaching "The Expansion of Christianity," a subject he referred to as his first love. He preferred that title to "Church History," favoring Kenneth Scott

---

33 McPhee, *Pickett's Fire*, 2001, 443, quoted in Parsons, 2012, 163.

34 Interview with Greg Parsons, August 30, 2006, 7, quoted in Parsons, 2012, 180.

35 Winter, "Winter Initiatives," 31.

Latourette's thesis that church history should be understood as the story of Christianity growing and expanding. Winter considered Latourette's seven-volume *History of the Expansion of Christianity* the second most important book to the Bible, as it traced the rest of the story of God's kingdom expanding in human history. Latourette emphasized the impact of Christianity on any new culture or region as well as the impact of that culture or region on Christianity.

Under its third president, David Allan Hubbard, Fuller Theological Seminary expanded beyond its original School of Divinity to include the School of Psychology as well as the School of World Mission. Winter's old friend Dan Fuller had returned there to teach as well. (He eventually became dean of the Divinity School.)

Dan soon became aware that his father had his eye on Winter through Winter's writing. In Dan's words, "So my father knew about Ralph and people could see that there was really a person who was going somewhere and going to do something big and great in the Christian world." [36] Dan saw from the day Winter arrived that Ralph was excited about his opportunity at the School of World Mission. Winter realized from the start that his new position was going to be one of learning, more than teaching, and this proved true. With all of its students—who were referred to as "associates"—coming to the school after field service, SWM was like a mass meeting place for experienced missionaries. Fuller later related that Winter, when asked how many students were enrolled, replied that there were 100 teachers and four to five faculty. Whenever an associate enrolled, he or she was interviewed extensively by Donald McGavran about his or her field experience, largely out of McGavran's own interest in maintaining an awareness of the world.

---

36 Interview with Greg Parsons, March 7, 2005, quoted in Parsons, 2012, 179.

Of the three faculty members and those who would join them, Winter was the person most involved in new initiatives during his time at SWM. His ideas rarely sparked interest in or involvement from the greater Fuller community. There were just too many of them! Some of his initiatives took hold and bore fruit, however. Years later, when President Hubbard listed ten important things that the faculty of the School of World Mission had initiated, seven of the ten were started by Ralph.

By 1969 the faculty at SWM had increased from three to five, the additional faculty members having been recommended by Winter. The school had been operational for four years and had put together a large collection of MA theses written by its "associates." For a while some of these were published through a commercial publisher, but mission books were not selling well, and the publisher was increasingly reticent to expend the effort. SWM would have to do its own publishing if these useful works were to be made available. McGavran asked Winter to take on the task.

With the help of Roberta and their four daughters, Ralph, in 1969, took on the challenge of starting a publishing business. The William Carey Library (WCL) was structured as a sole proprietorship. By contract, later in the 1980s, any profit up to 6 percent was to be shared fifty-fifty between the Winters and the U.S. Center for World Mission (USCWM); anything over 6 percent would go 100 percent to the USCWM; any loss had to be borne entirely by the Winters.

Named for the nineteenth-century Englishman who began the Protestant missionary movement, WCL became the source for published SWM theses. WCL also marketed certain of these works to other publishers for wider distribution.

An early volume that WCL published was *The New Englishman's Greek Concordance,* which adapted the *Strong's Concordance* set of numbers to the *Englishman's Greek Concordance,* the latter having been virtually unusable for over one hundred years because of the absence of a numerical index. Later this volume was further refined into *The Word Study Concordance* and its companion *The Word Study New Testament*. Ralph enlisted his parents, his wife and daughters, his Sunday school class, students at Bethany Missionary Fellowship in Minneapolis, Minnesota, and others to complete this major project which he had begun while in seminary twenty-five years earlier. Ralph believed that strongly in studying the Bible in the original languages and wanted to make it possible for non-Greek speakers. He even postponed the family camping trip for an "excruciating week," according to daughter Becky, in order to complete the project.

In 1969, Winter published his 650-page compilation, *Theological Education by Extension*. Two more books followed in 1970: *The Twenty-five Unbelievable Years*, a continuation of Latourette's church history, and the mission book *Warp and Woof*. These were released from outside publishers, with additional distribution through William Carey Library.

As with most Winter initiatives, the WCL project was well thought out and prayed over. Other faculty saw the need for it, but most doubted its ability to succeed financially. Even after several years of operation, Paul Winter told his brother he wouldn't give a "plugged nickel" for the business. Yet it succeeded, both as a source of valuable mission information and as a business venture. Roberta worked there full time for three years (until she lost her voice as the result of a doctor's surgical mistake). Daughters Becky and Linda contributed numerous hours without pay. The other daughters helped with mailings, accounting, and manuscript preparation. In 2000, when Roberta Winter gave an account of the publishing business, it was selling $800,000 worth of books per year and had paid the U.S. Center for World Mission $100,000 in management fees, largely because the Center promoted WCL through its publication, *Mission Frontiers*. No operating money had come from any source other than the Winter family. In fact, they sunk their meager life savings into the project to make it work.

During his tenure as dean of the School of World Mission, Donald McGavran had been concerned with the need to establish a PhD in the field of missiology. Fuller president, David Hubbard had promised McGavran the chance to offer this degree before McGavran agreed to establish the School of World Mission, in fact. Subsequently, Hubbard had put off the idea. He argued that (1) there was no evangelical, scholarly society to engage the community of scholars on the subject; and (2) no journal existed to communicate the discipline. All of the Fuller faculty agreed with McGavran about the need to offer the degree. Ralph and Roberta felt compelled to do something about it.

A meager scholarly society of missions already existed. The Association of Professors of Missions (APM) was organized in 1952. It focused on East Coast scholars. Gerald H. Anderson, president of Scarritt College for Christian Workers in Nashville, Tennessee, and a former Methodist missionary, attended an APM meeting in 1970 and was "astonished" that only fourteen people attended. He was dismayed that this might represent the future of mission studies in the U.S.; Anderson made Winter aware of the association and its pitiful status.

When Winter attended his first APM meeting, he "immediately perceived an absence of the main bulk of mission teaching and research in the meeting for so simple a reason [that] the original definition of membership excluded Bible colleges and other undergraduate schools where a host of active professors [had] been teaching hundreds of students for years." [37]

---

[37] W. R. Shenk and G. R. Hunsberger, *American Society of Missiology: The First Quarter Century* (Decatur, GA, 1998), 9, quoted in Parsons, 2012, 189.

Winter and George Peters of Dallas Theological Seminary convened a meeting to discuss establishing a broader group that would draw from evangelical, ecumenical, and Roman Catholic scholarship. They enlisted well-known missiologists and announced a meeting at Anderson's Scarritt College to be held just before the next APM meeting. There was some opposition by APM members who believed that the new effort was being made in order to put an end to their organization, which happened to be in the midst of its own evaluation. Winter and the others believed that, while the APM needed refocusing, their broader-purposed organization could actually help the APM. In 1972 the American Society of Missiology (ASM) came into being, and in 1976 it was admitted into membership in the Council on the Study of Religion. The first obstacle cited by Hubbard had been overcome. All that was needed now was to publish a professional journal.

In 1972, with his publishing background expanding, Winter negotiated the transfer to ASM of a small, quality publication called *Practical Anthropology* that was ceasing publication. Seeking to fulfill all of the publication's remaining subscription commitments, he replaced *Practical Anthropology* subscriptions with a new journal, which he called *Missiology: An International Review.* The publication debuted in January of 1973. Winter would act as its business manager for its first six years. Various SWM faculty would be its editors. Alan Tippett, with the respect he had in anthropological circles, served for the first three years, followed by Arthur Glasser (later dean of the SWM, and one of a number of faculty brought there by Winter).

Throughout his professorship, Winter enjoyed learning from his students with their practical experience in the field. Winter noticed, though, that he never heard reports about large swaths of the globe. There were many places in the world that had not been evangelized, and no one seemed to have any intention of going to these places any time soon.

Winter put the matter in his characteristically pointed way: "I was sitting there and realized that I could have one thousand more missionaries come through my classroom and I would never have a missionary from a place where no missionary had ever gone."[38] Christians were simply no longer moving into unreached lands or to unreached peoples. This concern would focus the remainder of Ralph and Roberta's lifetime work, while the School of World Mission continued stimulating missionary scholars to research and analyze existing church initiatives in their fields. It would be many years before "frontier missiology"—the study of how to reach totally unreached people groups—became an accepted field of study at any seminary.

The paper Ralph Winter presented at the 1974 Lausanne conference contained ideas that he had been working on for some time, because the missions community was hardly thinking about the unreached, much less trying to evangelize them.

In a 1973 presentation in South Korea, he noted:

> There are at least 2,150 million non-Christians in the world (400 million Hindus, 500 million Muslims, 800 million Chinese, plus others) as compared to 100 million Western Christians and 70 million Asian Christians. In order to reach these millions, we need to mobilize missionary forces which are not from the usual church-oriented modality type of missionary outreach.[39]

Even earlier, the Berlin conference of 1966 had focused on looking at the world in terms of peoples rather than just countries. A survey had been sent to mission leaders from around the world seeking a list of groups or cultures that were not being impacted by the gospel. From this list, World Vision had started the Missions Advanced Research and Communications Center (MARC),

---

38 Parsons, 2012, 194.
39 Ibid., 246.

which identified six hundred such groups, all of whom were less than 20 percent Christian. The question, as MARC's director, Edward R. Dayton, expressed it, was: "Will anyone put this vast amount of information to work?"

Following the 1974 meeting in Lausanne, Dayton would quote Winter in *World Vision Magazine*:

> Most of us are people-blind! Because we have lived most of our lives with people very much like ourselves, we tend to ignore people quite different than ourselves or to think them "strange." All over the world, differences of race, language and culture are generally considered a nuisance rather than a blessing. But the Bible is not people-blind.

Winter's Lausanne presentation would solidify the idea of reaching out to people groups within countries, even where national churches had already been established. It pushed him to the forefront of discussion among church and missionary circles worldwide. Much more importantly, these ideas constituted a personal imperative for Ralph. What would he do for these unreached billions, and how would what he had learned to date shape his response? How would he wrestle with that challenge?

Ralph's parents, Hazel & Hugo Winter

Ralph in his navy uniform; Roberta in her nurse's uniform

Ralph as "Daddy" with two girls

Guatemala: Ralph, Roberta & three girls

With first great-
grandchild, Sophia Lewis

Barb & Ralph

With Teen Mania students

Aerial view of campus

8

WAGERING EVERYTHING

The passion for the 2.7 billion unreached people in the world that Ralph Winter communicated so memorably at Lausanne sprang from the questions with which he was wrestling—his personal calling and its demands. As he stood before the Lausanne Congress, Winter was not only concerned about what the evangelical missionary community as a whole would do about the "highest priority," he was considering what he should do. Ralph never articulated a problem without considering its solution. In fact, Roberta Winter tells us that in the summer of 1974—the year of the congress—Ralph was already eyeballing the campus that would eventually become the U.S. Center for World Mission.

This became an abiding and even depressing concern. Soon Winter would be accused of being the type of megalomaniac who finds in his preoccupations the secret to the world's mystery. A few wondered aloud, who was he to think that the 2.7 billion were his particular problem? Ideas drove Ralph, though, not his ego. Some of his colleagues at Fuller Seminary advised him to see his writing and teaching as the best way to exert his influence. Winter was not the academic, however, who was content with influence. He had his father's drive to build—to engineer solutions others could apply.

Winter was finally coming to recognize that his character and gifts, as well as his experience, had fitted him for the roles of problem solver and innovator in the world of missions, and it was time to devote all of his energies to doing nothing less. Ralph and

Roberta decided to take on establishing a center to focus on un-reached peoples, almost in desperation because no one else seemed committed to addressing the problem, and they feared that Ralph's insights would soon be brushed aside and forgotten. In doing so, they inadvertently also built a platform that would enable Ralph's unique talents to be fully realized.

Even so, Ralph tried to avoid unnecessary risks, hoping to bridge from his current position into the role to which he felt he was being led. During 1975 and 1976, Winter had been part of an ongoing discussion of long-term goals for the school that was led by Ed Dayton of World Vision, who was a planning expert. Out of these talks, the idea emerged that a legally separate major mission center was needed—one that could be a functional annex to the SWM. This arm of the seminary might house special library collections, serve as the base for publications on missions, and be an umbrella under which other mission organizations might take shelter. It could provide computerized research services to mission agencies, host conferences, and be an incubator for new initiatives. As Ralph had noted a year before, a nearby Nazarene institution, Pasadena College, was moving to a new campus near San Diego, and their plant was available for purchase. In his mind everything was fitting together for this new project.

When Ralph saw that he could not persuade his colleagues to take the project on, he became the reluctant leader of this new venture himself, just as he had done with the publishing initia-tive, the William Carey Library. With the early initiatives in Afghanistan and TEE, Ralph had persuaded other colleagues to either take on the projects themselves or help him. Now leadership was falling to him alone, which was an uncomfortable change.

When Ed Dayton turned in his report to Fuller's administra-tion, its recommendations were turned down. The following decades would see Fuller become a financially stable institution, but in the 1970s its finances were precarious. At one point in Winter's time, the administration asked the faculty if they might withhold a portion of their monthly salary in order to cover costs. President David Hubbard had no desire to launch a new venture, with its extra staffing, equipment, and property costs, when Fuller's financial position remained anemic. The faculty knew about the financial condition of the seminary and offered to raise the money on their own, from sources other than those commonly tapped by the school. To the administration's mind, such fundraising would have been a crippling diversion from the faculty's proper role. They were told, in effect, to get back to their teaching and research.

That's when Ralph took complete ownership of the ideas that had been advanced for this "annex" of the seminary. There can be no doubt that McGavran and Winter were the driving forces behind the idea all along, and once Fuller's administration rejected the idea, that left Winter as the only one able to take up the project. Donald McGavran was elderly and in ill health.

Winter's own ideas for what was needed then came together in a new way—or so it would seem from Roberta Winter's comments in *I Will Do a New Thing*, the story of the U.S. Center for World Mission's founding. His ideas were so big, however, that even he found them daunting.

He foresaw a center for world mission that would turn his speech at Lausanne into a working institution. To reach the world's hidden peoples would demand mobilizing Americans in a new way, performing sophisticated research on unreached peoples so that mission agencies could form strategic plans to reach them, and educating missionaries and those who supported them in how to engage in cross-cultural evangelism.

The only way anything like this could be accomplished was for Ralph and Roberta to assume the role of founders of the new institution. Initially, this seemed too difficult.

From the spring into the summer of 1976 Ralph tried to forget about founding a new center for world mission, although he did keep an eye on the Pasadena College campus. His unwillingness to act depressed him. The twinkle in his eye that Roberta knew so well disappeared amid his brooding. Unlike his call to the ministry, which he finally reasoned out on the basis of his anthropological studies, this decision put Ralph in touch with the presence of God in a new and disturbing way. For the first time really, he seemed to have been moved in a way that lifted his reason to contemplate and be drawn toward a calling whose providence God alone could know. As with so many saints, he wasn't happy about it. Was this indeed the long-awaited fulfillment of his obedience to God?

Ralph wanted to talk the idea over with his colleagues that summer, but for the most part they were traveling and teaching in other locations. The one colleague at hand felt uncomfortable even discussing the idea.

Nevertheless, Ralph found himself ready to commit. He told Roberta, "I feel so strongly that God wants us to buy that campus and start a center that will stress the unreached peoples. I just can't shake this conviction. I can't wait any longer. I've got to move." [40]

Still, in keeping with the decision's extraordinary nature, they asked God for specific signs along the way as to whether to continue. Winter called a family council meeting, asking for Roberta's opinion and those of his three daughters who were still at home. Ralph explained that he would have no regular salary, to which Linda replied, "That's okay, Daddy, I'll eat cardboard if I must!" His family standing with him, Ralph faced his first test, that of a possible location.

Ralph and Roberta decided to investigate whether they might purchase the nearby Pasadena College campus that had been long in their thoughts. It had already been vacated, as the college had reconstituted itself as Point Loma College in its new San Diego location. They had no money in hand, having spent their life savings of $10,000 to start the William Carey Library. They had no institutional backing, from Fuller Seminary or anyone else.

---

40 Roberta H. Winter, *I Will Do A New Thing* (Pasadena, California: William Carey Library, 2002), 31.

They would make inquiries, though, about what was sure to be a multimillion-dollar transaction.

Winter paid a visit to the Nazarene district headquarters. His timing turned out to be critical. Meeting with district superintendent Paul Benefiel, Winter learned that the forty-member full college board was to meet the very next day to make a crucial decision regarding the campus.

A proposal had been made by an Eastern cult, the Church Universal and Triumphant, to lease the entire facility for the next two years, and the board meeting was to make a final decision as to whether or not to accept it. Many Nazarenes were opposed to the idea but, because the college needed money, the board was evenly split on the matter. Although he was in no position to make a concrete offer either to lease or buy the property, Winter was able to insert his idea for using the campus for his mission center in time to be considered.

Several days after the meeting, Benefiel contacted Winter with the news that the board had voted to go ahead with the two-year lease, but that they had struck the cult's proposed option to purchase the facility. Winter was elated. He had time now to put together financing, knowing the campus would be available after twenty-four months. The Nazarenes had also agreed to have the executive board meet with Winter to talk with him specifically about what he had in mind.

At that meeting, Winter laid his quickly gelled plans to purchase the campus before the board. He made clear to them he was not representing Fuller or anyone else. He made three bold requests, telling Roberta that the board's decision as to his terms would be a sign of whether God wanted them to continue. These three terms were their Gideon's fleece: (1) Ralph was not interested in buying the campus unless the college stopped selling the off-campus houses. Ralph already envisioned the rents from these houses offsetting much of the operational costs of the Center—to the point that it might even be self-sustaining. He would insist on the houses being maintained through many negotiations to come. (2) He wanted free space on the campus during the cult's two-year lease term. He planned to use this space as a place from which to raise funds. (3) He wanted a $1 million reduction in the purchase price.

Although the board members doubted Winter's ability to fund such an immense undertaking, they nonetheless listened sympathetically to his proposal. In the end, they agreed to stop selling the houses and to give Winter the requested space for $100 per month. Because of the nature of what Winter was proposing, the executive committee agreed to consider reducing the asking price, which was $8.5 million plus an additional $3.5 million for the off-campus houses. In the end, the full board refused to lower the price. They would want a down payment of $1.5 million. Later they agreed that that down payment could be made in two installments: $850,000 the first year and $650,000 the second. There would be an $8 million balloon payment due at the end of a ten-year mortgage, and any payments up until that time would be lost if the debt was not paid off in full. Satisfied, Winter would write later: "In taking the initiative in 1976 to found the Center, I have never in my life felt so clearly drawn by the living God to make such a radical decision, either before or since."

As his colleagues returned from their summer travels, Ralph began consulting with them about his plans. They reacted negatively for the most part, advising Ralph to stick to his writing and teaching. The Winters asked the faculty of the School of World Mission to their house for breakfast. The Winters were shocked at their negative response and the cold shoulder they almost immediately gave the couple. "Who do you think you *are*," one naysayer asked, "for speaking for the 2.5 billion unreached people?"

Right then, Ralph had to fulfill a speaking engagement for the Evangelical Foreign Mission Association. His address, "The Grounds for a New Thrust in World Mission," was essentially his apologia for the Center. The lack of such a center was one of the twelve deficits he named in the mission world as it then existed. The others, like the "untrained missionary" and the decline of lay involvement in missions, especially by women, were unfavorable conditions the Center might help remedy.

Not everyone would prove negative, though, especially Ralph's oldest and closest friends. As plans developed for the USCWM, McGavran and Wagner would stand behind him, as would Dan Fuller, who told him: "If God told you to do it, don't worry about what might happen to Fuller Seminary. God will take care of us."

Ralph felt Roberta and he had "crossed the Rubicon" during the first week of the fall semester when they told President David Hubbard of their plans. He immediately tried to talk them out of it and implied they were betraying the seminary. Hubbard was concerned for the school's image. [41] No professor, he thought others would reason, would leave a tenured position unless there was a problem. He also believed that if Winter made the attempt and failed, it would reflect badly on his seminary.

There was never any personal animosity between Hubbard and Winter, though. In fact, Hubbard always considered Winter a major asset to the school. Like all of Winter's superiors, Hubbard had trouble keeping his professor "reined in," but he was always proud of Winter as long as he was on his staff. In fact, he often cited projects Winter had initiated as major reasons to support Fuller. As with this and other ventures, Winter's leaders never doubted his integrity, just his wisdom. Yet Winter's bold step of faith— one of many—would be rewarded in the Lord's timing.

As an interim measure, Hubbard suggested Ralph not resign his professorship to begin his new venture, but take a leave of absence instead. Roberta Winter believed that Hubbard may have assumed that, within a short time, Winter would have had enough of his "hopeless dream" and would return to Fuller. She also believed that Hubbard may have been concerned that Winter's Presbyterian

---

41 Parsons, 2012, 195.

affiliation would cause competition for that denomination's resources. (The Presbyterian Church was, and remains, possibly the largest source of both income and students at Fuller.)

Arthur Glasser remarked years later that, while Winter was "completely loyal" to Fuller and SWM, he "had to be free from his schedule of courses to initiate things of one sort or another. And so, it was the greatest gift to Fuller and to the missionary movement when Ralph Winter broke away." [42]

As he began to conceptualize his new program, Winter wrestled with what it should be called. He wanted the name to reflect a center that would think of every aspect of world missions for a U.S. audience. The name "World Mission Center" fit, but some thought the name implied that it claimed to be *the* World Mission Center. He settled on "U.S. Center for World Mission," making it *a* center, not *the* center. As the years went by, Ralph would be gratified to see similar institutions spring up around the world, among them the Singapore Center for Evangelism and Mission and the University of Edinburgh's Centre for the Study of World Christianity.

Winter's conception of the Center's mission and his vision for its programs were both remarkably cohesive and varied. He initially saw all of the programs as being staffed by missionaries on loan from other mission agencies. As the need for staff became urgent, however, it also became clear that he needed to establish a focused core community, which came to be called the Frontier Mission Fellowship. The essential task of the Center would be to address unseen or neglected obstacles to mission and devise solutions that would address the roots of the problems so that these remedies could be applied, not just in one locale but globally. The desire to get to root causes, even if other people were skeptical, would stay with Winter for many years, and through many issues—not all of them related to world mission. The Center's programs, however,

---

42 Interview with Greg Parsons, February 10, 2005, quoted in Parsons, 2012, 194.

generally fell into one of three areas: (1) strategy, (2) mobilization, and (3) training.

At its founding, the Center focused on the urgent need to retool the mission industry to reach unreached people groups. That is still its primary emphasis today.

The essential charisma of the Center—its main contribution— always went beyond this, however, as it reflected Ralph's gift of seeing what was missing in the effort of God's people to spread the kingdom of God. This essential genius began opening up new avenues to be pursued, late in Ralph's life and still today.

One can readily see the roots of the Center's emphasis on research and education in Ralph's personal history. From his days in seminary when he taught the Christian side of history to USC undergraduates, Ralph had tried to address educational gaps. Lausanne proved him the master of the statistical research that his colleagues Tippett and McGavran did so much to foster. His concern for mobilizing Americans to engage once more with mission came out of experience that built momentum in the 1960s and 1970s.

In the early 1960s a wave of nations, especially in Africa, declared independence from their colonial rulers. Missionaries in these lands suffered a good deal of violence and were threatened with much more. This caused mission agencies to retrench as they became eager to hand over their charitable institutions to nationals. America's war in Vietnam seemed to many the unhappy result of our own colonial desires. Even those in America who supported the war found the ultimate futility of the effort a reason to let the world solve its own problems. The 1960s also brought an aggressive secular challenge into Christian homes. Churches became preoccupied with dealing with the hippie generation and the sexual revolution. The 1970s were the "Me Decade," as Tom Wolfe described these years, a time when the American church was as inwardly focused on personal problems as the surrounding culture. The Ladies Missionary Circle, a staple in evangelical churches from the turn of the century, virtually disappeared. The yearly missionary conference, with its witch-doctor rattles and grass skirts, seemed an embarrassment in a postcolonial age.

Winter had made a special study of the Student Volunteer Movement for Foreign Missions that sent thousands of missionaries abroad in the late nineteenth century and early twentieth—many packed their belongings in coffins so that if disease or violence took them, as it did many, they could be more conveniently shipped home for burial. Where had that type of Christian dedication gone? How could it be restored?

In 1973 the annual InterVarsity Urbana Convention drew four-teen thousand college students to what would become a watershed meeting in the history of Christian missionary service. Interest in missions on college campuses had been waning for years, and although Urbana attendance had grown, the percentage of attend-ees signing commitment cards was declining every year. By 1970 only 8 percent of the attendees were willing to commit to service. However, the 1973 meeting, the largest ever, saw commitments jump to 28 percent.

When Winter learned that InterVarsity had no follow-up plans for these thousands of potential missionaries, he asked InterVarsity's permission to contact each student about attend-ing a summer missions course of his own design, in order to keep them interested in missions. It was now January 1974, and no one thought he could possibly put such a course together by summer. InterVarsity was not in favor of giving out the names and address-es of its Urbana attendees, and conference head David Howard tried to put Winter off by making it clear that his idea was hope-less. He asked Winter five questions, four of them directed to how much work would be needed and the fifth to the all-important, bottom-line question: "Who will hold the bag, financially?"

Over the following two weeks, Winter made some two hundred phone calls and had answers for all of Howard's questions, includ-ing the last. A group of mission executives from across the country

agreed to sponsor and hold the summer program at Wheaton
College. At this late date, though, many could only devote a single
week to teaching that summer. Rather than turn the list over to
Winter, InterVarsity agreed to send out their own letter of inquiry
to the committed students. Only two students responded.

With his sponsors in place, Winter urged his two oldest daughters (now in college at UCLA and Caltech, and both planning to
attend the program) to get on the phone every morning before 8
a.m. and call students who, through various means, had expressed
an interest. At Winter's request, Billy Graham offered to announce
the program twice on his *Hour of Decision* radio broadcast. Harold
Lindsell, one of Winter's Fuller Seminary professors from back in
1947, ran a full-page article-announcement in *Christianity Today.*

With time so short, it was a wonder that anyone signed on.
However, twenty-nine enrolled for the first of the two proposed
sessions of what later was called the Summer Institute of
International Studies. All of them were excited by Winter's courses.
Seizing that advantage, Winter stopped the whole program for
one day and assigned the students to write and call friends to sign
on for the second session. The effort brought in enough additional
students, allowing the program to break even.

In typical fashion, Winter quickly lined up someone else to run
the summer program after the first few weeks, while he set about
creating a legal governing board for future seasons. He would,
of course, watch the program's financial accounts no matter who
was in charge. The second summer included a four-week trip to
Guatemala, as well as a special session for those who had attended
the previous year.

The summer course would continue, eventually becoming the
successful mission education program now known as Perspectives
on the World Christian Movement. This college-level course
has been taken by over 100,000 people in North America alone.
Over 200 classes are held all over the U.S. with an average yearly
attendance of 7,000. In addition, approximately 18,000 have taken

Perspectives in some 700 classes outside the U.S. The basic text of the course, *Perspectives on the World Christian Movement,* co-edited by Winter, is an 800-page volume addressing the crucial aspects of missions. Besides being used in the Perspectives course itself, it's used widely in seminaries and colleges as a standard missions text. The program began in a humble way.

Winter made his final decision to separate from Fuller Seminary on October 31, 1976, though at the president's suggestion he remained on unpaid leave for a while longer.

Criticism continued. Some of Winter's closest friends tried to convince his first five board members to remove themselves in order to avoid involvement in the future legal consequences following the project's "inevitable" failure. He was perplexed that his best friends in the ministry would give him no word of encouragement, not realizing that they wanted no blame for the impending disaster. While most would say nothing, some others, Winter recalled, indicated their doubts by asking, "How does your wife feel about this?"

Of course, it was Roberta and their daughters who gave Winter the most earthly encouragement. He wrote later, "I look back on those moments of decision as almost a dream." [43]

Ralph and Roberta endured the criticism and went on because they knew how vital their mission was. As Ralph famously insisted, "Risks are not to be evaluated in terms of the probability of success, but in terms of the value of the goal."

Because they saw what others did not, they had hope. As Ralph's colleague Donald McGavran taught: "We are not in the sunset of missions, but the sunrise."

---

43 Winter, "Antecedents to the Founding of the U.S. Center for World Mission," *Frontiers,* 9.

On November 5, 1976, Ralph and his family incorporated the U.S. Center for World Mission. Winter had only a price tag from the Pasadena College board. No contract or agreement had been signed.

It would be January before one USCWM board member insisted they offer the Nazarenes $15,000 to hold their option to purchase the campus, and even that amount was unavailable at the time. The board member offered to put up $5,000 if the other $10,000 could be found. Several days later, completely out of the blue, a donor to Lutheran Bible Translators wrote out a check for this amount upon hearing it was needed. The $15,000 was offered, but elicited no response. As it turned out, the cult had suddenly offered a "huge amount" (according to Winter) for its own option to purchase the campus—a sum rumored to be $75,000. Although a verbal agreement had been made not to option the property for sale to the cult, its new offer changed some minds among the Pasadena College board. Months went by with no answer from this board.

James Dobson had founded Focus on the Family that same year and was well known to Nazarene circles. He wrote a letter to the Nazarenes telling them that if they went back on their word in favor of the cult, he would announce it to his entire southwest radio constituency. (Or so Winter was told. He never knew for sure whether this letter was actually written; within a couple of days of his hearing that it had been, he received his signed purchase option.) It was now March 1977. He had until September 1 to come up with $850,000. He had lost three months waiting for the board's reply.

Even with time incredibly short, Winter was unwilling to go to the public for money until he had a list of outstanding mission leaders on his letterhead. He began a relentless weekly letter-writing campaign to forty-five such people (most of them personal acquaintances) eliciting their support. Leighton Ford of the Billy Graham Evangelistic Association offered support, but only as a consultant, not as an advisory board member.

Taking the hint, Winter began using that term in his solicitations. All but one agreed to be listed as "consultant" on the Center's letterhead.

This accomplished, Winter went into action. It was now June, the deadline to raise $850,000 less than three months away. He and the board had the Fellowship of Artists in Cultural Evangelism, a member agency, produce a brochure, which it printed in large numbers and air freighted across the country.

In three months Winter and the Center collected $450,000, including $50,000 from philanthropist Howard Ahmanson. A fundraiser headlined by the 1950s crooner Pat Boone brought in more than $25,000. At the last minute, the USCWM received its tax-exemption letter, and the Ahmanson Foundation donated another $105,000 toward the total.

Still more than $300,000 short, Winter and his board overcame a reluctance to borrow. (Winter believed that borrowing money should be reserved for instances where real property could be put up as collateral.) Winter received three loans of $100,000 each: one from his friend Bill Bright's organization, Campus Crusade for Christ; another from World Literature Crusade; and the last from the same board member who had given the $5,000 toward the purchase option. Still the Center was short of the total amount on October 1 (it had been previously given a one-month extension). Winter and his supporters bargained for a week's extension for the rest. This was granted. The Center was also given more lenient terms as to the second down payment of $650,000, which was delayed until September 1, 1978. In this and many other instances, the Point Loma College officials showed themselves flexible, extending grace, while remaining good financial stewards.

Donations continued to come in, and the Center met its full obligation of $850,000 the following week, on October 7. To make this possible many gave sacrificially, including missionaries and college students. One church whose building had burned down even shared a large portion of the insurance payment, believing God would bless for this act of faith.

In the following three months, the U.S. Center paid off the one loan that carried interest and began repaying both Campus Crusade and its angel investor. Ultimately, Campus Crusade generously forgave $60,000 of the U.S. Center's loan.

Most of the staff wanted to keep raising funds toward the $650,000 second half of the down payment, wanting to avoid another round of financial brinksmanship. Winter insisted, though, that the Center start into its proper work while continuing to raise funds, likening the task to building a boat while sailing. Now, not even the analogy's strong suggestion of drowning gave him pause.

9

"YOU WILL SAY TO THIS MOUNTAIN"

As a first program, Ralph Winter thought the U.S. Center for World Mission ought to offer a class in world missions that college students might take during the interterm month of January. This was modeled after the Summer Institute of International Studies program that Winter began in 1974. He asked Bruce and Christy Graham to run it.

Bruce had been trained in aeronautics at Oregon State University and earned an MS at MIT. He was among the first participants of the Summer Institute and became one of Winter's students at Fuller, receiving an MA degree in cross-cultural studies. While at Fuller he was a resident of "The Haggai Community," a forerunner of the Frontier Mission Fellowship, the community that staffs most of the U.S. Center's programs. He would be one of Ralph's right-hand men during much of the rest of Winter's life, and continues serving at the Center. As a fellow scientist, Bruce has always understood Ralph as few others. In addition to running the interterm course, Bruce and Christy launched a related program called World Awareness Seminars for local churches.

In May of 1977 Ralph learned that the Summer Institute of International Studies was failing. Not enough students had signed up to cover expenses at its University of Colorado location. Most of the young staff who had gathered around Winter at the Center came out of this program—the Winters' daughter Beth had even met her husband, Brad Gill, there. The Center stepped in to save the program. Under Brad Gill's leadership, the staff recruited

thirty students and ran a January (1978) intensive program out
of the postage-stamp digs the Center occupied on the former
Pasadena College campus.

The Summer Institute of International Studies, as well as other
fledgling efforts like the World Awareness Seminars, evolved over
time into the Perspectives on the World Christian Movement
course with its *Perspectives* text. This hallmark program of the
U.S. Center became a dynamic means of mission mobilization
and recruitment, reengaging the evangelical church in the cause
of missions. Its chief merit lies in its approach to the Bible. One
might expect a text about today's missions to present a broad overview of what's happening around the world, describing the latest
developments, opportunities, and challenges. Instead, the text first
addresses the reasons for mission, as well as historical analysis, and
uses contemporary material in the context of case studies. What's
most striking is the way the Bible is presented as the story of
God's mission in the world.

In the twentieth century, evangelical Protestantism became
almost exclusively about personal salvation. It defined itself over
against liberalism and its social gospel. For evangelicals, the faith
was not about social amelioration; it was about a one-on-one encounter between God and the individual mediated by Jesus Christ.

This theology worked well enough in terms of missions for
the age of William Carey and Hudson Taylor because evangelical Protestants believed in hell in a heartfelt way. Taylor could
speak of millions of Chinese being doomed to eternal punishment
because they had never heard the gospel.

During the latter half of the twentieth century, evangelicals
still believed in hell, but more as a matter of a necessary, if perplex-
ing, doctrine than an abyss at one's feet. It became impossible to
motivate anyone to take an interest in people in foreign lands by
talking about hell.

In the 1980s and thereafter a few evangelical thinkers began
reclaiming the whole world as God's concern—both creation and

humankind. George Ladd, Lesslie Newbigin, and N. T. Wright launched what came to be known as "kingdom theology."

After all, Jesus announces his ministry by proclaiming the kingdom of God is at hand. The word "kingdom" can also be translated as "rule." God's way of doing things is about to appear, and indeed it does in Jesus' person and ministry. Jesus concerns himself with people's circumstances, their illness, their poverty, their grief, as he demonstrates God's love and invites his hearers to love God in return. He means to defeat the "strong man," Satan, and occupy territory that would otherwise be under Satan's rule. The church on earth—the church militant—is an occupying force until Christ's return and the resurrection.

Kingdom theology seeks to reunite the corporate and individual aspects of the gospel, transcending the modernist divide of conservatives and liberals. The work of reconciliation entrusted to the church includes social amelioration as well as personal salvation, because Christ's kingdom is characterized by justice and peace as well as communion with God. Jesus embraces us with one arm in friendship and the other arm as Lord.

The announcement of God's kingdom—his will to restore all things—begins in God's covenant with Abraham. God promises Abraham that through him "all nations/peoples on earth will be blessed" (Gen 22:18; 26:4; 28:14). From Abraham to the people of Israel to Jesus Christ and his church, the Bible is a missionary saga—God's tireless work to reclaim his creation as well as fallen humankind from the devil.

Mission is the Rosetta Stone—the interpretive key—to the Scriptures, to the history of the church, and to each believer's role in God's plans. If a person chooses to follow Jesus, he or she joins God in mission.

This does not necessarily mandate that everyone become an itinerant preacher or travel to a foreign land, but it does entail each Christian working to enlarge the kingdom of God and beat back the rule of Satan, whether at home or abroad. It also entails the understanding that mission is not something the church may elect to do; mission belongs to the nature of the church. Winter said, "The essence of the Church is missionary."

The Perspectives course has evolved over the years, but its delivery system still resembles the model Winter and his colleagues adopted for the TEE program. It is usually taught in local churches where various experts give three-hour presentations one night a week for fifteen weeks. Students prepare through self-study materials that accompany the *Perspectives* textbook. As with the TEE program, the Center brings its Perspectives course to where people live and enables them to do the work on their own time. Although many people take the class just to be informed, undergraduate and graduate credit can also be earned.

The Perspectives course is part of the U.S. Center's efforts to *mobilize* the evangelical community for missions. New initiatives were badly needed to replace the Ladies Missionary Circle and missionary conferences, which in many churches had become a thing of the past. So other mobilization programs soon emerged from the U.S. Center.

One was the magazine *Mission Frontiers*. Now published every two months, *Mission Frontiers* is at the forefront of the global movement to establish an indigenous church among the world's ten thousand unreached people groups. The magazine has a circulation of over eighty thousand subscribers in more than one hundred and sixty countries. Numerous people have encountered Ralph Winter and his writing for the first time through *Mission Frontiers*. Many clergy and other Christian workers read this periodical primarily to understand their own roles within the body of Christ, as well as informing themselves about issues related to missions and particularly unreached peoples—its articles and commentaries are that rich and multifaceted.

Another mobilization effort that began almost immediately at the U.S. Center was the *Global Prayer Digest*. Ralph and particularly Roberta understood that people are far more apt to be moved by concrete examples than abstract thinking. The Winters knew that we would never reach the unreached if they didn't get people praying. The *Global Prayer Digest* provides a snapshot of a specific unreached people every day.

In one instance mobilization took a literal turn. At Roberta's suggestion, after reading about Joshua, Ralph called on the U.S. Center's staff to join him in another "march around Jericho"—a demonstration march around the Pasadena College campus on successive Sundays. These marches were conducted in a prayerful spirit with hymn singing. They finished near the deadline for the first down payment with a march that circled the campus seven times, just as Joshua and his men did before the walls of Jericho came tumbling down. The marches attracted publicity, as Ralph knew they would, and motivated people from surrounding churches to take up the U.S. Center's cause as their own. Winter's purposes ran far deeper, though, than merely the manufacture of publicity.

At the time the old Pasadena College campus was occupied by the Church Universal and Triumphant—or the Summit Lighthouse, as it was also known. Ostensibly "Christian," the cult embraced a mix of Hindu and Buddhist teachings. It most closely resembled the old spiritualism of the late nineteenth and early twentieth century; it invoked a variety of "ascended masters" who then directed the cult's activities through its leader and chief medium, Elizabeth Clare Prophet.

The cult continued its attempts to buy the Pasadena College campus from the Point Loma College board, and clearly saw the U.S. Center as its enemy. It conducted spiritual warfare against the U.S. Center by chanting before a giant Buddha installed in the former Nazarene college's main auditorium. During the Jericho demonstrations, the cult broadcast classical or Christmas music to drown out the marchers' hymn singing, and once tossed raw eggs from an upper-floor dormitory window, splattering marchers.

As Ralph Winter's call to found the U.S. Center marked a new stage in his spiritual life, so the challenge of the cult, especially in the context of the seemingly impossible fundraising task, provoked responses from Winter that relied on faith-based solutions. He was much more visibly putting on the whole armor of God, in order to withstand all the wiles of the devil. Roberta and he, as we've seen, began talking about crucial events as "fleeces," remembering how the Old Testament hero Gideon discerned God's will. In *I Will Do a New Thing,* Roberta writes of the spiritual oppression the U.S. Center's staff felt as the result of the cult's chanting against them. In response, the staff kept long prayer watches.

Ralph's sense of life as a spiritual battle deepened. He was wrestling not only against flesh and blood, but against principalities and powers and the rulers of the air. It was an emphasis that would continue to the end of his life.

The cult's opposition sharpened Ralph's sense of the spiritual battle in which the U.S. Center and his family were involved. He thus embraced approaches to fundraising that were grounded in God's sovereignty. These methods were often frustrating to his staff, maddening to his board, and deemed crazy by development professionals. Ralph and Roberta thought fundraising techniques ought to be part of God's leading—a mix of practical wisdom, taking good advice and, above all, understanding our utter dependence on God.

As others have in Ralph's position, he received contradictory advice from the various professional fundraisers his board and others constantly sent his way. He shouldn't aim at raising the down payment of $1.4+ million. That would inspire no one! He had to put the whole 15-million-dollar vision before people at once. He could not do that, though, because he did not have an adequate mailing list. No one could raise the type of money needed to secure the future of the U.S. Center without a deep mailing list and a long history of contributions. His only hope was to get large foundations involved or a handful of wealthy individuals. Did he know of any? If not, what was he up to?

In response to well-meaning but ultimately confusing professional advice, Ralph went with his heart. What he really wanted,
and what he thought God wanted, was for the U.S. Center to
ignite a new movement of interest among evangelicals in global
missions. Ralph was not aiming at launching a handful of programs.
Whatever programs the U.S. Center ran, the much larger goal
was to inspire this popular movement. If the Center only proved
a demonstration project that caused others to embrace the *cause*
and carry it forward more successfully, that was fine with Ralph.

His fundraising initiatives reflected this ultimate goal. They also
kept the larger missions community and its needs in mind. Ralph
never wanted the U.S. Center to compete with other mission
agencies for funds. Its success depended on other mission agencies
regarding the Center as a friend and partner. Ralph's first appeal
was democratic to its core. He estimated the total cost of the campus and its houses with interest would be $15 million. The Center
could raise this sum if one million evangelical Christians gave $15
apiece. Donors were asked to include another ninety-five cents to
cover the mailing costs of the book Roberta had just released about
the Center, *Once More around Jericho;* a pie chart showing *Hidden
Peoples;* and a six-month subscription to *Mission Frontiers.* These
were sent as a thank-you. Roberta's book proved—and has ever
since—the best fundraising tool the Center has ever possessed.

Ralph took practical steps to publicize the $15 campaign,
contacting Billy Graham and the publisher of *Christianity Today,*
Harold Lindsell, and his other contacts throughout the world.
He enlisted the help of mission agencies, who published news of
the campaign in their publications. He wrote a "grapevine letter"
that supporters could pass along to others. Ralph and Roberta
made barnstorming fundraising trips throughout the country to
raise awareness of the U.S. Center and its needs. In the end, the
$15 campaign fell well short of providing the necessary funds to
meet the second down payment of $650,000. Others contributed
much larger gifts, however, and the Center was able to meet its

down payment obligation on September 1, 1978. The one rule of professional fundraising that proved roughly true—as far as I can determine—is that 20 percent of the donors eventually contributed about 80 percent of the total down payment amount.

Still, Ralph was determined that any larger gifts should be considered a loan and the money either repaid or used in a "revolving fund" to help other mission endeavors.

The U.S. Center was finally able to occupy the entire former Pasadena College campus that fall.

The Church Universal and Triumphant first decamped to "Camelot," a 218-acre property in the Santa Monica mountains, before moving on in 1986 to Montana, where it eventually succumbed to its leader's Alzheimer's disease and fractious rivalry.

Long years of mortgage payments lay ahead for the U.S. Center and what eventually became two final balloon payments of $8.5 million for the campus and $2.3 million for the surrounding housing. That hardly deterred the work, however.

Visitors to the U.S. Center's affiliated William Carey International University (WCIU) arrive at a location that looks like a college campus, with a legacy central building roofed with Spanish tile and topped by a clock tower, a rectilinear stucco and glass library out of the 1960s, a cafeteria, smaller classroom buildings, and California-style apartment complexes that serve as dorms. This seems fitting as so much of the U.S. Center's efforts over the years have been devoted to education, including the World Christian Foundations curriculum as well as William Carey International University.

What's confusing, though, is the minimal number of students on the grounds. The place is a beehive of activity, with multiple schools and organizations occupying office space and a small contingent of students in residence, but the gaggles of undergraduates talking their way across the lawns, the loungers catching their rays, the skateboarders swooping around pedestrians, and the more solitary grad types with their leather briefcases are largely absent. It actually takes a while to understand the nature of William Carey International University and the U.S. Center's other educational programs and how these relate to what the visitor sees. Most of the WCIU students are spread out in locations around the globe. Much of the U.S. Center's building is occupied by other ministries and organizations, as Winter always intended. William Carey International University occupies enough space for its programs while its staff conducts operations across the world, with students in every hidden corner of the globe.

Winter founded WCIU with the needs of "scholar-activists" like himself in mind. He wanted to fulfill his dream of offering universally credible degrees, an MA and PhD in international development. He again wanted to deliver this education to students where they were—this time to missionaries and NGO workers in the field. As wonderful as he knew the School of World Mission at Fuller Seminary to be, Ralph knew that few missionaries and NGO workers who would benefit from advanced degrees could take the time needed to attend a seminary in the United States. Winter believed that he would not be competing with the Fuller Seminaries of the world because his students would have no chance of availing themselves of such opportunities. (One can see, of course, that the same students who might have thought of coming to Fuller before the advent of William Carey International University would find Winter's institution far more convenient and never make the effort. This may have motivated some of the resistance at Fuller.)

In order to make his highly specialized university work, Winter knew that with his colleagues he must accomplish two goals: he must design an integrated curriculum that would tell the whole story of God's action in the world, and the education component must include original research.

As a student at Caltech, Ralph found out how inadequate his
education had been as to the beliefs of many of science's greatest figures. It was not long before he was trying to supply the
Christian side of history for students at the University of Southern
California, only to find out that graduates of the preeminent
evangelical college, Wheaton, whom he thought might help him,
knew as little of that side of the story as those at USC. At Fuller
he taught church history as the ongoing work of God in reclaiming humankind and creation from the devil. Throughout Ralph's
life, from his boyhood when he found the will of God his own key
to learning better and faster, he tried to put together the whole
story of God's action in the world.

Once the U.S. Center became a reality, Ralph began devoting
years, along with his co-workers, to producing an integrated curriculum that would tell the whole story of God's redemptive work
throughout time—a curriculum that would be flexible enough
to serve as the basis of a BA or MA degree. Through a massive
amount of work undertaken in the 1990s, the World Christian
Foundations curriculum finally came into existence. It originally
encompassed more than 400 books and 1,000 articles by 300
different authors.

The World Christian Foundations (WCF) curriculum invests
the traditional liberal arts curriculum with "a broad, 4,000-year
global, mission perspective." It makes Jesus' kingdom theology
the golden thread holding everything together.

The WCF curriculum would become the basis of the MA
degree in international development offered by William Carey
International University. Employing Ralph's favorite learning
techniques, this MA degree combines a great deal of self-study
under a mentor who meets regularly with the candidate. The
WCF curriculum is also offered in an abbreviated form as an
online single-semester course that students can take with others
from around the world. It has also been made into the year-long,
thirty-six-credit INSIGHT (Intensive Study of Integrated Global

History and Theology) course for college students. An early forerunner of this integrated curriculum, developed by Winter's second daughter, Rebecca Lewis, serves as the basis for the K-8 Judson International School curriculum and the popular *Sonlight* homeschool curriculum.

Winter knew from personal experience that PhD programs consist mostly in mentoring relationships and original research. William Carey International University could function as a highly specialized PhD-granting institution to missionaries and NGO workers in the field if mission agencies in the field and NGOs, many of whose staff members possess a PhD, would become the partners of WCIU. Instead of candidates applying for the university's PhD program, the holder of a PhD within a mission agency or NGO would suggest to a co-worker that together as mentor and student they pursue a PhD program. This would benefit the agency by commissioning original research and the candidate by opening new doors for service.

Although delivered in an unusual way, both the MA and PhD degrees of William Carey International University were rapidly granted "full institutional approval" by the State of California. Winter always remembered fondly that a member of the state approval team remarked, "Your PhD requirements are tougher than Stanford's."

The educational component of the U.S. Center is complemented by original research. The Center publishes the *International Journal of Frontier Missiology* for the International Society of Frontier Missiology—an academic journal devoted to describing unreached peoples and promoting a conversation among mission leaders about how they can best be reached. Members of the WCIU faculty, U.S. Center staff, and other recognized missiologists as well as pastors and lay people are invited to contribute to this quarterly journal.

From the beginning of the U.S. Center, this research component has also involved data mining of global demographics. Through this means the Center has been able to provide mission agencies with a current picture of the unreached peoples to target.

As the work of the U.S. Center went on, Ralph, Roberta, and their co-workers endured a decade and more of financial brinksmanship. Through several subsequent renegotiations with the Point Loma College officials, the final balloon payment on the campus of $8 million became due in the fall of 1987—eleven years after the Center began. A subsequent payment of more than $2 million for the houses around the campus would be due a year later. It wouldn't be until 1989, in fact, that Ralph Winter would be completely free of his ministry's debt as he neared his sixty-fifth birthday. This was a strange burden to bear for someone almost fanatically frugal with his personal finances.

In the intervening years, Ralph had been engaged in a long struggle to maintain ownership of the approximately 150 homes and apartments around the campus. Ralph's board, seeing the ministry struggle, suggested at several points that the U.S. Center sell off some of this campus housing, either to pay down the indebtedness directly or to raise cash in order to tear down some of the houses and rebuild condos that would command higher rents. At one point Ralph was forced to cede to this demand. The sale of the housing was only stopped by the Point Loma officials themselves, who pointed out that the U.S. Center had no right to sell what they as yet did not own. Ralph heaved a sigh of relief, because he always envisioned a day when rents from the housing would make the ministry self-sufficient.

Still, at the beginning of 1987 the U.S. Center had only $1.3 million in cash and pledges toward the $8 million balloon payment. One of the Center's staff members, Bob Coleman, came up with the idea of the "Last $1,000 Campaign." This came out of a telephone conversation in which he asked a potential donor whether he might give $1,000 if the donor knew that his $1,000 would end the fundraising effort and secure the campus. If he knew that, the person said, he would most certainly contribute $1,000.

The "Last $1,000 Campaign" demanded that close to 8,000 people each donate $1,000. Ralph's board was actually relieved that he was finally asking for more than $15. A general appeal with a colorful brochure went out all across the country. By this time, as a result of the $15 campaign and other efforts, the Center did have quite a mailing list. Ralph gave the "Last $1,000 Campaign" teeth by promising that all the money that came in would be put in escrow. If the campaign failed to raise the full amount, all contributions would be returned.

This ignited people's enthusiasm. Ralph and Roberta soon realized, however, that the numbers still seemed overwhelming. What might work better would be to have individual $1,000 donors recruit two or three people to donate as well. Most people in a position to donate $1,000 know at least that many people who might join them.

The U.S. Center stayed in regular communication with its donors. Having once sent out a general appeal, the Center now concentrated its communication efforts on those who had already become donors, updating them frequently on the number of "Last $1,000 Campaign" donors needed. This built momentum. Still, four weeks from the October 1 deadline, the campaign was $5 million short.

As the deadline approached, the board rebelled, with some insisting that all the money be returned. One board member said he had not signed on for an indefinitely continued campaign—that was not the promise made. Ralph thought there might be a third alternative between no deadline and an indefinitely extended deadline. The promise he had made was that the money would be returned if all the money was not raised—not necessarily by the original deadline. Once again, Ralph negotiated with the Point Loma College officials for an extended deadline. With all the payments the U.S. Center had made to date, and seeing that the ministry did have several million dollars in hand, the Point Loma officials gave the Center until the end of the calendar year.

Students gave $1,000; missionaries gave $1,000; others provided much larger gifts. Close to New Year's Day, one woman promised to make up any remaining difference. "Shortly after noon on December 31," Roberta writes, "we had all we needed, or at least what we thought we needed. Those manning the phones were still trying to answer several at once. But the rest of us were running around the corridors, praising God and hugging each other." [44] As Roberta indicates, there were still wobbles to come, mostly due to pledges that were late in arriving.

On January 16, 1988, however, 1,500 friends of the U.S. Center gathered to celebrate the victory. The U.S. Center would endure. Ralph Winter's pipe dream turned out to be visionary.

The leaders of struggling organizations are often left to their own devices, but once an organization becomes a success, controlling it becomes much more desirable. Four of the U.S. Center's board members now became, in Ralph's phrase, an "indigestible lump" to the board's functioning. They quarreled with every decision and mandated meeting after meeting.

Those who supported Ralph pointed out the desirability of having the four contrarians resign. There was a face-saving mechanism at their disposal, one that might avoid the unhappiness of direct confrontation. The board had been discussing reformulating itself into three three-year "classes," with the term of one class expiring

---

44 Winter, *I Will Do a New Thing*, 318.

each year. In order to do so, the whole board needed to resign, except Ralph, who would then reconstitute the new board into these classes. Ralph reappointed all but the dyspeptic four.

The face-saving gambit worked only in part. The unhappy board members went to the evangelical press and made the board's collective resignation seem a rebellion against Ralph's leadership. Several misleading articles were written, including one in *Christianity Today,* the evangelical magazine of record.

No one likes to be embarrassed in public. When Ralph wrote about this episode, though, he described the incident with even-handed realism. He did not fault the motives of the men with whom he had clashed. He stated directly that they were fine Christians and people of goodwill. He cited the incident as a case in point of how Christians with the best intentions in the world sometimes have serious disagreements. This was not Ralph "taking the high road"; it was more than that. His concern seemed to be for other Christian leaders, his own community, and young people. He wanted his audience to know that such things happen in Christian organizations so that they could be prepared. Perhaps he was thinking back to Ruth Wardell in Guatemala and no doubt similar stories he heard from many of his one thousand students at the School of World Mission. His remarks were wise and calm and came out of a genuine humility.

After the 1990 fracas, the U.S. Center, with the board, enjoyed a decade of producing and implementing its landmark programs. Globalization began directing the attention of Americans to other nations, particularly China and India. Likewise, the Western church began thinking again at last about her far-flung brethren in the global South, as the phenomenal success of Philip Jenkins' *The Next Christendom* would prove in 2002. The U.S. Center was at the forefront of a massive cultural shift.

And Ralph? Ralph began thinking about other, even more difficult, questions.

10

IS THE TERROR OF CREATION
GOD'S WILL?

A s the culmination of Winter's work, he took on the most difficult question in theology, the problem of evil (theodicy), with its agonizing extension in our lives—unmerited suffering. How should we understand the nature of disease and respond to its devastating effects as God's cocreators? What accounted for the neglect of disease eradication, Winter asked, as a mission field for believers?

In 1996 Ralph's wife, Roberta, was diagnosed with multiple myeloma, bone marrow cancer that was already present in more than one location. Myeloma develops when plasma cells responsible for producing antibodies that help destroy infection become abnormal and begin manufacturing M proteins. Once the myeloma cells begin dividing rapidly, they make the victim subject to infection, anemia, bone pain, bone loss, kidney problems, and heart problems.

No one knows what causes myeloma, although risk factors may include being exposed to certain chemicals or germs (especially viruses), genetic variances, eating certain foods, and even being overweight. (That Ralph would be diagnosed in 2002 with this same disease suggests that the couple may have been exposed to a common environmental cause or viral pathogen.)

At the beginning of her illness, Roberta was diagnosed through an MRI that found a one-inch-long tumor in her spinal column at T7–T8. She had been feeling tired, and an annual physical exam detected non-iron-deficiency anemia. A few weeks later she experienced crippling pain on the right side of her back that radiated to the front, which was caused by the tumor. She speculated that the carpal tunnel syndrome that she had suffered from the year before in both wrists might also have been related.

Myeloma has no cure. There are treatments that can cause the disease to go into remission for periods of time, including chemotherapy, steroids, radiation therapy, and stem cell transplants. These treatments cause problems of their own, and a battle with myeloma means difficult years of gradually deteriorating health, with chronic pain.

Roberta fought hard against the disease. She was remarkably capable, by virtue of her training as a nurse and her disciplined life, of seeing the progress of her myeloma with clinical detachment, as in the case history she wrote for the Myeloma Foundation as a help to others and research. As her daughter Tricia recalls, however, "She was heart-sick from the first day of the diagnosis through the next seven years."

Winter turned his fertile mind and fearless questioning to the problem of evil and disease in a world God had lovingly created. Not content with the usual answers offered by Christian apologists, he characteristically began digging for root causes, as well as what the proper response ought to be.

In the fall of 2001, as America was thrown into confusion by the September 11 terrorist attacks on New York's Twin Towers and the Pentagon, Ralph kept vigil by Roberta's bed as she succumbed to the disease.

Roberta always described being married to Ralph as holding on to the tail of a comet, but Roberta fueled Ralph's velocity in virtually every project, from the Hebrew lexicon they worked on together in seminary to grading papers and teaching at times for his classes at Fuller to the high-risk U.S. Center for World Mission venture. The book that Roberta wrote about the U.S. Center's founding, first titled *Once More around Jericho* and in subsequent editions, *I Will Do a New Thing*, aided the ultimate success of the Center. Roberta's conversational, heartfelt style helped a large, general audience, many of whom might have been mystified by Ralph's intentions otherwise, connect with the Center's mission and make it their own.

As Roberta lay dying, Ralph contemplated losing the woman he loved, the mother of his children, his chief collaborator, his best spokesperson, and someone who was fiercely protective of his achievement. In *I Will Do a New Thing* Roberta recounts how she had to learn not to take criticism of Ralph so much to heart. It was better—more freeing—to leave Ralph's defense in God's hands.

Nevertheless, in the year 2000 Roberta wrote a perceptive profile of her husband occasioned by criticism that Ralph "ought to bow out of all administrative functions and 'do what he does well, writing and speaking.'" Ralph would later joke that Roberta "defended him" by saying he wasn't much of a writer or speaker. What she said was that these talents were subordinate to his main gift: the ability to see needs others did not and invent ways to meet those needs. She writes in her profile:

> What he initiates is not done to gain recognition or esteem but rather to initiate whatever he can to "destroy the works of the devil" (1 Jn 3:8). For this simple reason alone he has by God's grace seemed to be able to endure opposition, ridicule, slander, etc., as have many other leaders who also have initiated something new, for whom the gleam of foundational accomplishment has been more important than human recognition. [45]

How would he ever continue his work without such a fiercely loyal and gifted woman by his side?

During the first twenty-eight days of October 2001, Ralph thought about the "big" terrorists on the world's mind right then

---

45 Winter, "Winter Initiatives," 1.

and the terrorists too small to see with the naked eye that were killing his wife. The 9/11 Islamic terrorists killed close to three thousand people, but millions died each day as the result of disease. Why did people not have the same "lurid awareness" of these microscopic terrorists as they did of Islamic terrorists? He wondered in particular about why the church had not devoted its attention to the eradication of disease. Acknowledging that in the past Christians had devoted tremendous efforts to treating and caring for the sick, even curing disease, Winter still questioned why the church had not addressed *eradicating* as many diseases as possible.

"Our theological heritage," Winter writes, "begins to stumble at the question of our declaring war, in the Name of Christ, on all disease, and seeking the total *eradication* of all disease-causing pathogens." [46] Winter went on to point out that the discovery of DNA and the efficacy of modern medicine brought with them new responsibilities. Given the availability of such tools, looking to prayer alone as the Christian response became a refusal to follow Christ in his healing ministry. He compared it to praying for God to paint the back fence when a brush was handy.

Roberta Winter died on October 28, 2001. Ralph could not help but wonder whether—if the church had been truly obedient to her Lord in the area of disease, Roberta's cancer and the Alzheimer's disease affecting his friend Robertson McQuilken's wife, Muriel, and the heart disease that took the evangelist John Wimber too soon—all these diseases might have been virtually eradicated long ago from the face of the earth, like smallpox.

Ralph Winter's mind went to work on these questions in a way typical of his genius. He took the facts before him and then he "reverse-engineered" how they came about, as when a computer

---

46 "The Story of Our Planet: Origins, Evil, and Mission," *Frontiers*, 220.

company, not wanting to infringe on a competitor's patent, takes a new product, pulls it apart, and figures out how the product works. In this case he was "reverse-engineering" Christians' strange indifference to the eradication of disease as a godly calling.

Or, to use another analogy, Ralph went to work on the problem like a detective solving a murder mystery. A detective reasons backwards from the "what" of the story (the murder) through the "how" (the method of the crime, like strangulation) and the "why" (the crime's motive, like greed or passion) to the "who" (the culprit).

Ralph could not solve the mystery of myeloma, but he could solve it with the "crime" of the church's neglect of disease eradication. If he could solve the theological mystery at hand, scientists and physicians might be encouraged to tackle the eradication of disease with new vigor as their Christian calling. Pastors in churches might help inspire this through their teaching. Unbelievers would no longer confront a Christian God who appeared indifferent to people's suffering and death, which might open the minds of millions to the gospel—the real gospel.

What he noted first was that Christians were reluctant to talk about disease as a manifest evil.

They certainly prayed for God to cure disease and had built countless hospitals and sent medical missionaries by the thousands to respond to the effects of disease in the world. This implied that disease was contrary to God's will—to the One who "forgives all your sins and heals all your diseases" (Psa. 103:3). Serious disease leads to death, and death is the final enemy that Christ will destroy (1 Cor. 15:25,26). We see in Christ a Savior who comes to give us "abundant life," as well as life everlasting. Jesus' healing ministry prepares for the resurrection. Each miracle is a small enactment of the ultimate victory over death Christ experienced in his own flesh.

In Genesis, death comes into the lives of our first parents, Adam and Eve, by virtue of their sin, not God's expressed will.

Christians today rarely speak of disease as an evil opposed to God's will; instead, they finesse the subject by counseling the seriously ill to accept affliction as if it came from God's hand. In "A Growing Awareness about Disease," Ralph cites Philip Yancey's story about five Christians who visited the hospital bed of a woman named Claudia. [47]

The first visitor said that God would never have inflicted such a disease upon her if there weren't unconfessed sin in her life. The second banished anything negative with an insufferable cheer. A third visitor thought if Claudia simply believed enough she would be healed. A fourth counseled Claudia to see herself as a spiritual athlete, whose testimony, despite her suffering, would show forth the transforming power of faith. Claudia's pastor confessed that we do not always know God's purposes, but Claudia needed to be able to say, "Thank you, God, for this disease." That would show she was capable of belief without knowing all the answers (a counsel that raised the ante on "spiritual athleticism"). No one was willing to say that Claudia's disease might have an evil source other than Claudia's own sin.

"In no case," Winter writes, "did anyone say, Satan is behind this."

Winter laid much of the blame for how Christians understand disease at Saint Augustine's door. Reacting against the dualism of his Manichaean period, according to Winter, Augustine sought to emphasize God's sovereignty. He "failed to understand disease and violence as something (1) not only within God's sovereignty, since 'He has not ceased to rule from the galaxies to the atom,' but (2) *essentially the initiative of a superhuman, evil person.*" [48] Traditionally, theologians have drawn a distinction between God's perfect will, his sure purposes, and God's *permissive will,* in which God allows for the possibility of evil in order to grant some of his creatures—the angels and humankind—free will. Orthodoxy

---

47 Winter, "A Growing Awareness about Disease," in *Frontiers,* 176.
48 Winter, "The Story of Our Planet," *Frontiers,* 220–221.

across the Christian communions is founded upon the absolute goodness of God as theology's first principle. Winter believed that this principle had effectively been compromised.

For Winter, Christians were far too disposed to chalk up to "God's will" the existence of premature death, tragedy, disease, and even "violence and gruesome cruelty." Winter thought the willingness of contemporary Christian apologists to see an autistic child, for example, as "just the way God wanted him to be" radically mistaken. The child might teach those who loved him lessons about the nature of God and humanity, but this was only because God can use the evil of a child's impairment (as well as the image of God in which the child was made) for God's greater glory, just as God used the death of his only Son to bring about good. Autism, like other diseases and disorders, should never be considered part of God's perfect will.

Accepting disease as "God's will" leads people, at best, to an unhealthy acceptance of evil, and at worst, to outright apostasy. Winter strongly believed that genuine Christianity has refused to believe in a God who causes disease and destruction; such beliefs have resulted in a terrible passivity to the outright evil of disease, where strenuous action is called for.

He described this mistaken emphasis on God as the author of all things as syncretistic and fatalistic. He saw it as a perversion of the idea expressed in Romans 8:28 that "all things work together for good" (KJV). He viewed such acceptance as an institutionally sanctioned "theological blind spot."

Few Christians have trouble seeing the unmerited suffering caused by disease as an evil, I would suppose. They simply don't know how to connect their understanding of an absolutely holy God with what they see before them in hospital rooms. The problem has become acute as we have grown increasingly timid about connecting the evil we see in the world with the biblical source of evil, Satan. Even the most conservative Christians have grown leery about ascribing anything to the devil. The evil one has become simply a horned, pitchfork-bearing cartoon figure in red tights despite the four Gospels in which the battle between Jesus and Satan forms the essential conflict.

Satan, Winter states, has given us a "double whammy: A demonic cultural delusion piled on top of a demonic physical distortion!" [49] The devil has convinced us of his irrelevance or nonexistence in order to perpetrate his crimes against creation unopposed.

The worldview of Western Christians has become so immersed in the dominant thinking of the surrounding culture that we believe only in what we can experience with the five senses, with careful exceptions. Among these are the reality of prayer, personal regeneration through the Holy Spirit, the miracles of Christ, and his resurrection.

The supernatural contest between God and Satan that pervades the Scriptures, however, has become alien.

For this reason, Ralph and those who were close to him theologically, like Lesslie Newbigin, Stanley A. Ellisen, John Stott, and others, sought to reclaim the fully supernatural context of the Scriptures.

Ralph emphasized in particular that two rebellions set the stage for the biblical drama. Christians commonly speak of the Fall when discussing how Adam and Eve alienated humankind from God by eating forbidden fruit. Prior to Adam's sin, though, one of God's angels, Lucifer, mounted a rebellion against God, attracted a third of the angelic host to his side, and was expelled from heaven (Rev. 12:4–7).

Because of his rebellion, Lucifer (which means "light-bearer") became Satan ("adversary"). Satan's rebellion against God was the first of the *two falls,* and the way God responds to Adam and Eve's sin cannot be understood apart from this background.

The continuing relevance of this Old Testament background to Jesus' ministry can be pointed out through its salience in Jesus' life.

---

49 Ibid., 202.

After the inauguration of his ministry, Jesus *immediately* retreats into the desert, where he prays and fasts for forty days. There he undergoes Satan's three temptations, resisting Satan's entreaties to pursue power, fame, and glory. Only after this supernatural contest does Jesus begin confronting his earthly opponents, the Jewish religious authorities and Roman officials.

The Synoptic Gospels virtually teem with demons. The demons recognize Jesus' true identity as the Messiah long before his followers. Seven major episodes in the Gospels relate to Jesus' exorcisms. The Gospels cannot be understood on their own terms without acknowledging their supernatural worldview in every aspect—not simply where we choose to do so for the sake of maintaining salvation history.

Jesus' parable of "binding the strong man" teaches that he has come to bind the "ruler of this world," as Satan is described in another passage, in order to take possession once more of the house of creation and its inhabitants. In a passage Ralph appealed to again and again, John underlines the point: "The Son of God appeared for this purpose, to destroy the works of the devil" (1 John 3:8 NASB).

The contest between Jesus and Satan pervades Christian tradition. Medieval and Renaissance paintings of the Crucifixion often included a mouse trap at the foot of the cross. The Father trapped Satan like a mouse when he allowed the devil to put his Son to death. Then Jesus used Satan's own deadly means against him when Christ arose from the dead and proved his power over Satan.

The Apostle Paul tells us that we fight not against flesh and blood, but "against principalities, against powers, against the rulers of the darkness of this world" (Eph. 6:12 KJV). He also witnesses that "the creation was subjected to futility" (Rom. 8:20 NASB)—nature itself was cursed by sin—and groans to enjoy the marvelous freedom of the children of God.

Ralph liked to quote the Dutch theologian G. C. Berkouwer, who said, "You cannot have a proper theology without a sound demonology."[50] Ralph saw that Christians were giving up in the fight against Jesus' intelligent opponent, Satan, because they did not believe in Satan—not in their heart of hearts.

Once we take off our Western blinders, we can see that from the beginning of the Scriptures in Genesis God's *mission* is to respond both to the fallen angels and to man's sin. Simultaneously, he intends to reclaim his creation and to redeem humankind.

In Genesis 3:14,15 God addresses the serpent first: "I will put enmity between you and the woman, and between your seed and her seed; he shall bruise you on the head, and you shall bruise him on the heel" (NASB). This passage is referred to as the "proto-evangel," the first announcement of Christ's good news. It prophesies Jesus' victory over Satan, as he will crush the head of the serpent, but not before Satan inflicts a lesser wound on Jesus— bruising him "on the heel"—as he's put to death on the cross.

Stanley A. Ellisen writes, "Thus in this proto-evangel in Eden, God introduces, in outline form, his twofold program for his king- dom and man's redemption. He would ultimately reclaim his total kingdom by destroying Satan and Satan's kingdom, and would redeem believing men in the process by the death of Christ."[51]

God's judgment in Genesis includes nature: "Cursed is the ground because of you; through painful toil you will eat food from it all the days of your life. It will produce thorns and thistles for you" (3:17,18). But the completion of the work of Christ, as the Apostle Paul tells us in Romans 8:21, will see "creation itself ... liberated from its bondage to decay and brought into the freedom and glory of the children of God."

---

50 Winter, "A Blindspot in Western Christianity? Its Meaning for Mission," *Frontiers,* 201.
51 Stanley A. Ellisen, "Everyone's Question: What Is God Trying to Do?" in *Perspectives on the World Christian Movement: A Reader,* 4th ed., ed. Ralph D. Winter and Steven C. Hawthorne (Pasadena: William Carey Library, 2009), 19.

This is the heart of Christian tradition as it applies to our understanding of the two falls and their consequences.

Ralph also saw a strand in the tradition that he thought might be teased out further. If God announces Jesus Christ's advent while pronouncing judgment on Adam and Eve, if he is already preparing to defeat Satan and redeem humankind, then the entire story of the Bible is about God's mission in human history. Not just from Abraham on, as he chooses a people from whom Christ will spring as Savior of the entire world, but right from the very beginning.

Winter then asked a speculative question about which there is no direct biblical answer, although there may be, as he believed, an indirect biblical evidence as to its answer. He wondered whether God might have created men and women to be his allies in reclaiming creation. Had the garden been implanted in order to counter Satan and the fallen angels? Why, after all, did God bring men and women into existence? What if Adam and Eve had not sinned? Would they still have had a role to play?

If Satan appears as a serpent in the garden, could the fallen angels have been actively at work in precincts outside of the garden of Eden? It might be the case that the earth already hosted a fallen creation outside the garden. So Eden may have been a reclamation project. God places his co-workers—made in God's own image—on the earth to facilitate his retaking of creation from Satan. That's their purpose—their mission—from the beginning.

This plan is complicated by Adam and Eve's rebellion but not finally thwarted, because God is willing to *become man*—as the second Adam—in order to be at once humankind's redeemer and Satan's conqueror. Man in Christ accomplishes the first Adam's mission.

The whole story of the Bible should be seen, Winter believed, as God's attempt to reclaim his creation from intelligent evil, assisted by humanity. It's the story of God and humankind's mission against the rebellious angels.

Other respected Christian thinkers have had the same idea, among them C. S. Lewis. "It seems to me … a reasonable supposition," Lewis wrote, "that some mighty created power had already been at work for ill on … planet Earth before ever man came on the scene … If there is such a power, as I myself believe, it may well have corrupted the animal creation before man appeared." [52]

Ralph Winter thought the idea of the garden being contemporaneous with a fallen creation worth pursuing; it opened up the possibility of the biblical account of creation and today's scientific account being reconciled. He began rethinking what Genesis and science tell us.

---

52 C. S. Lewis, *The Problem of Pain*, (New York: HarperCollins, 1962), 138.

11

VICIOUS CREATION

The way Christians in our time finesse questions about the evil of disease, Winter came to believe, reveals even more about the state of contemporary Christianity than an overemphasis on God's sovereignty. It is also a way of preserving a role for God, if an impoverished one, in an age of science.

The scientific mentality resists accepting God's intervention in human affairs. This derives from the way science is done as it seeks to establish how the universe works as verified by empirical data. The tremendous success of science inspires the common assumption that nothing may ultimately lie outside science's explanatory power. More than a few take an obvious intellectual pride in how the achievements of science justify, they feel, their own atheism. Stephen Hawking, Richard Dawkins, and a whole crop of "new atheists" make this case.

Even the outstanding physicist and Anglican priest John Polkinghorne in books like *Science and Providence* prefers an immanent God, a God in whom we live and move and have our being—as opposed to an interventionist God, one who acts directly in human affairs. In his heart of hearts Polkinghorne would prefer, it seems, to narrow God's direct intervention in human history down to Christ's resurrection. He sees the Resurrection as a singular event more than the guarantor of God's power to act directly in human history at any time through miracles and prayer.

Polkinghorne's philosophical caution finds its garden-variety cousin in the reluctance of many evangelical Christians to regard disease as anything more than the natural order taking its course; one that becomes a spiritual concern only as God uses it in people's lives for the sake of spiritual growth.

Because what's the alternative?

In his later writing Winter put forth a bold alternative, one that pitted what he saw as a truly biblical worldview against science-as-religion and the skittish Christianity of those avoiding the scientific steamroller. It's among the most interesting and farsighted ideas he advanced, and it came toward the very end of his life, not in the middle period of the Lausanne years. That's why his greatest influence as a thinker may only be realized in the future.

Ralph's alternative makes troubling imaginative demands, though; it stretches our thinking in ways that disturbed even some within his own community. He freely admitted the hypothetical nature of his thinking. For Ralph that was the point: to address problems that were going wanting for lack of independent thinking that could then be considered thoughtfully by the whole Christian community. *That was who Ralph was.* After a lifetime of zeroing in on this elusive identity, he used virtually every moment of his last years to live it out without compromise, and without regard for the consequences.

Unlike many of his colleagues in missions and the clergy, Ralph wasn't afraid of scientific thinking; it was his first intellectual milieu. He also had such an unusual confidence in his God that he wasn't worried about looking around some scientific corner and finding that God had disappeared.

When Winter began thinking about how Christians regard disease as opposed to the scientific view, he went straight at the problem by collecting the evidence and seeing where it led. Many

Christian thinkers want only a place at the table of contemporary thought; Ralph was confident God had created and owned any table worth occupying.

As he looked at the problem, Winter noted, as everyone does, that science has one narrative of how the world works; Christianity another.

The universe is a vast machine, says science, born in the instant of the big bang, operating according to chance. The world is indifferent to the desires of humanity except insofar as these have adaptive value. The "scientific story" is not strictly science, as everyone admits, but the inferences people tend to make from what science has discovered.

In the Christian story God creates the world out of nothing and invests it with an order that reflects God's own personhood: God's truth, goodness, and beauty. Nature speaks of God's love for the human person, a creature made in God's own image.

Since Darwin, much of Christian thinking has been devoted to reconciling a personal God who shapes human history for God's own purposes with a universe whose processes appear purposeless. Purposeless at best, for so much of the way the world works metes out unmerited suffering to humanity through disease and cataclysm. Winter was fond of citing statements by Darwin in which Darwin claimed that evolution by natural selection actually preserved God's reputation, given the crimes against humanity of which he could otherwise be accused. [53] Why would a loving God invent typhus, amoebic dysentery, cancer, and cyclones? Darwin thought it possible—although how honest he was being about this is a question—to maintain the idea of a creator who then became essentially irrelevant and thus maintained a degree of innocence.

As to typhus, dysentery, and other natural horrors, the Christian response has grown increasingly to be: we don't know, but God can

---

53 See Winter, "Where Darwin Scores Higher than Intelligent Design," in *Frontiers*, 191–94.

use it for good somehow. It is almost as if Christians have become fatalistic, denying God's power to intervene for good in human affairs and the natural order.

That didn't satisfy Ralph Winter. He thought the weakness of the answer a prime reason why so many Christian young people lose their faith during their college years.

Ralph also thought it a peculiar proposition to proclaim a loving God to the world's non-Christians, only to admit that this loving God wasn't powerful enough to address their afflictions.

Could the narratives be synthesized? Or was one simply wrong, the other right?

We know that Winter's quest for answers to this question started with watching his wife, Roberta, die of myeloma. Whatever redemptive consequences might come of this event, the event itself was a manifest evil.

This steered Winter away from a common explanation of how to reconcile the scientific and Christian narratives. Ever since Darwin, some Christians have attempted to supply the Darwinian corpus with a Christian soul. Christians claimed that natural selection was simply the mechanism that God used to accomplish his purposes, all the while guiding and shaping natural selection and adaptation to God's ultimate purposes.

All that guiding and shaping must have gone terribly awry, Ralph must have thought, when it came to myeloma.

There's also a technical problem for any Christian who looks honestly at the latest understandings of neo-Darwinian theory. According to the theory, not only is natural selection and adaptation random—without any guiding purpose or hidden "soul"—but it must be in *principle* in order for the theory to be valid. Chance or randomness is an essential part of the theory—take it away and the whole theory falls apart. To read the neo-Darwinian literature with intellectual honesty, one must come to the conclusion that the theory, as it presently exists, cannot be baptized with holy

purposes. Chance is as essential to neo-Darwinian theory as it is
to the Pick-6 Lottery.

After a lifetime of devoted Scripture study, Ralph knew the
importance of Satan's fall from heaven and how it preceded the fall
of Adam and Eve. He began with a conviction as to the certain evil
of disease and an inkling that the way in which we read Genesis
might be inadequate. If he brought these insights to what science
has to say about creation, might he find something others had over-
looked or neglected? He would, as at the new campus of Westmont
College, make a survey, this time of two different intellectual
terrains; then overlay his maps and see if there were surprises.

As a scientist himself, Ralph was less inclined than other
Christians to doubt the intellectual integrity of scientific findings,
although he was careful to distinguish the data from philosophical
inferences made on their basis. Many Christians resist science's
basic finding that the earth is millions of years old. A whole school
has grown up around "creation science," which has widespread
acceptance among American homeschoolers, and teaches that
the earth is only thousands of years old and what purports to
be scientific evidence to the contrary is radically flawed. In his
writings Ralph always made due acknowledgment of this position
and noted that some within his own family believed this. He also
traced the lineage of "young earthers" back to Ellen G. White and
the Seventh Day Adventists. He simply found the evidence for an
old earth far more compelling and trustworthy.

As he studied Darwinian theory as it exists today (usually
called neo-Darwinian theory), he found the great anomaly that
neo-Darwinians such as the late Stephen Jay Gould took such
pains to address. As originally conceived, Darwin's evolutionary
theory posited that life developed in a smooth, continuous line
over millions of years from a single-cell organism to the grand
diversity of the animal kingdom as we know it.

Neo-Darwinians know this is not the case. It took a long, long time, neo-Darwinian theory teaches, for single-celled organisms to develop and for these to develop further into multicelled invertebrate creatures. (Invertebrates still account for 97 percent of all life forms.)

Then, quickly in evolutionary terms, complex vertebrate creatures suddenly appear in what is known as the "Cambrian [era] explosion." Not only do a whole new range of species appear during the Cambrian era, but for the first time nature becomes decidedly "red in tooth and claw" as many species are carnivorous. Species begin to sport protective mechanisms such as horns and armor like skeletal structures in order to fend off predators. As the world turns vicious, it also turns parasitic, with many forms of new invertebrate life springing up which survive through bringing injury or death to their hosts.

How did this happen? And why? What accounts for the Cambrian explosion? Why does the "record of the rocks" present us with eras that continue for millions of years with little change and then, suddenly, change radically? Can evolution speed up and slow down? If it could, why would it?

Scientists now generally agree that the history of the earth's development has been radically altered—"punctuated"—across the eons by major asteroids colliding with the earth. These collisions interrupted the stable patterns of life on earth and precipitated relatively quick evolutionary changes in the earth's life-forms.

This belief was given much of its impetus, as Winter notes, after the United States landed on the moon and its craters were found to be the result of asteroidal impacts rather than volcanic eruptions. Science then went on a hunt for evidence of asteroids colliding with the earth and found such evidence in abundance. A number of asteroids were several miles in diameter—one of the largest found to date hit Mexico; large enough to bring on "nuclear winters," involving global climate change and the destruction of most existent species.

According to neo-Darwinian theory, life rallied from these set-backs by evolving far more rapidly in response. This was made possible not only by natural selection and adaptation but also the new element science was coming to understand as underlying these, gene mutation. Evolutionists adopted the phrase "punctuated equilibrium" to describe what it now found to be the earth's history of long periods of relative evolutionary stability, punctuated by asteroidal cataclysm, followed by rapid evolutionary development, before the earth once more settled into evolutionary stability.

The theory of "punctuated equilibrium" claims that because new life-forms were needed and needed in a hurry, they therefore developed—in a hurry. Why would a blind process whose major theme is stability and whose minor theme is change suddenly change character after a cataclysm? At a minimum, the "blind process" would have to be not so blind but in some way sense need or have an inner directive. But sensing need and having inner directives indicates intelligence of some type, if only the type of intelligence displayed by programming. How could what, we are constantly told, must be a *random, mechanical process* be programmed to operate one way under one set of conditions and another way given new conditions?

Programming requires a programmer, and that brings some type of god back into the picture, either as a collective intelligence (pantheism) or as a person (the Judeo-Christian God).

Ralph found the exclusion of God from the scientific narrative nonsensical. He liked to use the analogy of how the automobile has developed from its Model T days to today's hybrid SUVs and the alternative-fuel vehicles of our future. The automobile has certainly evolved, but as the result of thousands of engineers around the globe redesigning its structure year after year.

At the time Ralph Winter was thinking about life's origins and the implications of evolutionary theory for theology—and specifically, the Christian understanding of disease—the school of "intelligent design" had already done a great deal of work posing arguments that questioned whether evolution really could be a random, mechanical process. If it could not be, as the thinkers associated with intelligent design came to believe, to what degree could evolutionary theory be considered valid?

(Parenthetically, it needs to be pointed out that the school of intelligent design is *not* an offshoot of creation science, nor a stalking horse for "young earthers," nor an attempt to replace science with theology. Creation science and the intelligent design movement are constantly conflated in mass media—particularly by the "reliable spokesmen" of those who find in evolution a justification for atheism.)

The most renowned thinker to emerge from the intelligent design movement is Michael Behe, the author of *Darwin's Black Box*. He questions how the many complex structures necessary for life could have evolved through small, incremental steps. How could a complex structure like the eye, for example, have come into being one piece at a time? Half an eye is useless. The lens or light-receiving cells of the retina have no evolutionary advantage without every other part of the eye functioning as well. Every structure in an eye must be present for these individual structures to be of any value.

To explain what he means, Behe uses a simple mousetrap as an example. A mousetrap consists of a wooden base, a spring-loaded catch, and the wire bar that traps the mouse. Each of these elements alone has absolutely no ability to catch a mouse. They all have to be present and in the correct configuration in order to serve the intended purpose. There are literally thousands of structures in one human cell that have this same property of what Behe calls "irreducible complexity."

As an engineer Ralph Winter saw Behe's point and applauded the intelligent design movement.

He thought its insights should be taken several steps further, however, because the questions about the nature of creation only began with random process versus intelligence. There remained the question of the *nature* of this intelligence. In Genesis God pronounces all of his creation "very good," but much of creation as we know it is far from good. In fact, it's malevolent.

Could God's good, intelligent design have been corrupted by the malevolent designs of other intelligent creatures? Was this in fact the biblical picture?

Ralph thought it might well be. He looked closely again at the creation account in Genesis 1. There the light is separated from the darkness *before* the creation of the sun and moon. In English, Genesis begins, "In the beginning God created the heavens and the earth" (1:1). A more accurate translation of the Hebrew, however, may be: "In the beginning, when God was refashioning or re-creating the heavens and the earth." Because the next sentence—"Now the earth was formless and empty, darkness was over the surface of the deep, and the Spirit of God was hovering over the waters" (1:2)—does not describe a situation of "nothingness" as much as a radical confusion, a situation in which it's hard to tell which side is up.

The next verses clarify as God separates the waters, producing the sky and an expanse of water below, and then drawing these waters into the seas so that the dry land appears. Ralph asked whether Genesis might have been produced out of a distant memory of an earthly cataclysm—a time when an asteroidal impact in the Middle East might have produced a "long winter," a time of near total darkness and flood—before conditions returned to normal. That would account for the light appearing before the sun and the moon, because the sun's light would have created day long before the solar system's star could actually be seen.

Ralph's speculation about the genesis of Genesis gains in credibility for me because other pieces of ancient literature describe similar origins. For instance, Homer's epic poems, *The Iliad* and *The Odyssey*, were long thought to be purely fictitious without any historical referent until 1871, when Heinrich Schliemann established the historical site (if not the proper strata) in modern-day Turkey at Hissarlik. [54] Schliemann's find was based on the work of Frank Calvert, a British archaeologist who had been working on the site for twenty years.

One can easily imagine that a similar process to the creation of Homer's epics had been involved in the writing of Genesis—a historical event gave rise to a long oral tradition that was then codified for its theological import.

The time Genesis 1 references might be around 12,000 to 10,000 BC, and it's the case that the Middle East experienced a major meteoric impact at that time. [55]

The story of the garden of Eden comes from Genesis 2. It follows what's often called a second creation account, a shorthand referencing of God's creation of the heavens and the earth and streams coming out of the ground to water the land and make it fruitful. Genesis 2 also gives us another account of God's creation of man and woman and says directly that God "planted" a garden in a particular location for their home. Winter looked at how the story later unfolds and found accounts—such as the stories of giants, the Nephilim, descended from the "sons of God" (usually thought to be fallen angelic beings, or demons), and references to the people that the accursed Cain will be wandering among—suggesting that the garden was planted amid a preexisting, surrounding creation.

Not only C. S. Lewis accepted this possibility, but so did the patriarch of nineteenth-century evangelicalism, C. I. Scofield. The notes Scofield supplied to his edition of the Bible served generations of evangelicals as a guide to orthodoxy.

The scientific story and the Christian story might be reconciled, Winter reasoned, by supplying what was obviously missing from

---

54 See Wikipedia, "Heinrich Schliemann," http://en.wikipedia.org/wiki/Heinrich_Schliemann.

55 See Winter, "Impacts, Eruptions and Major Mass Extinctions," in *Frontiers,* 223–24; Winter, "Making Sense to Today's Scientists," in *Frontiers,* 240–43; Winter, "Planetary Events and the Mission of the Church," in *Frontiers,* 290–91; and Winter, "The Unfinished Epic," in *Frontiers,* 317–26.

the scientific story—intelligence—and a recasting of common assumptions about Genesis, one that other well-known authorities had entertained.

Winter proposed that the two stories aligned in the following way. When the first fall occurred at the rebellion of Satan and a third of the angelic host, God exiled them from his presence in heaven. They sought revenge by seeking to corrupt God's creation. Their rebellion might have occurred about the time of the Cambrian explosion when vicious forms of life and countermeasures to this viciousness—such as immune systems—appeared on earth. We find in the Bible that it's part of God's character to invite his creatures to be cocreators of the world with him. God also gives his creatures free will. This is straight orthodoxy. So Winter wondered, why should this not apply to the angels? Perhaps the angelic hosts had a role as the first engineers, working with God through millions of years to develop the biodiversity of the earth.

Is it possible that the fallen angels may have stayed at the same task, but now in a new mode, seeking vengeance against God by designing life-forms that brought violence and death to God's good creation? In turn, angels loyal to God sought to protect God's creation by designing defensive mechanisms against predatory, parasitic, bacteriological, and viral forms of life.

God planted Eden and created Adam and Eve in order for them to assume control of God's project to reclaim his creation from the *malevolent design* of the fallen angels. This project was impeded by our first parents' own rebellion against God, but not finally defeated, because God in Christ would come through the chosen nation of Israel to redeem humanity and restore its cocreative, redemptive mission. From the very beginning, then, men and women were meant to help God heal God's creation. Predation, violence, and disease have always been evils humankind was meant to help undo. Thus, the Great Commission, to "make disciples," can be seen as the same as that task given to Adam and Eve, "multiply and subdue the earth."

Winter's vision was a grand one, and clever, certainly, but is it only one more crackpot theory among others? Winter was an incredibly smart man—"God's genius," as I'm calling him—and also levelheaded. He knew how his reconciliation of the scientific data and Christian story would sound to most. It sounded that way to people within his own organizations, the Frontier Mission Fellowship and the U.S. Center for World Mission. Winter never expected his staff or anyone to buy into his thinking in these areas. He knew it was speculative. But he also knew that it was important for believers to honor God by recognizing his original purposes in creation.

He chose to print a reply to his theory in his own book, _Frontiers in Mission,_ from a critic who states more politely the crackpot accusation. This correspondent objected that Ralph's thinking must always remain unproven speculation and hoped that it did not represent the official position of the organizations with which Winter was associated. Otherwise, the worrier could never participate.

Winter replied calmly that he completely understood the speculative nature of his theory, and again, _that was the point_. How else could unanswered yet vital questions be addressed if not through floating out novel ideas for others' consideration?

He also delved with his colleagues and correspondents into why the mind rebels at the notion that both intelligent and malevolent design were involved in the planet's history. The problem derived from our resistance to a robustly supernatural worldview. Like Polkinghorne, we'd rather God not demand too much of us in regard to what many Christians—even the stoutly orthodox— fear to be the Bible's unwarranted supernaturalism.

I can hear many protesting, "No! No! We are all on board with that!"

Really? I'd propose that it's more the case that orthodox Christians like myself are fond of Jesus' miracles and are ready to give our lives for a doctrine like the bodily resurrection of Christ, but when it comes to the many exorcisms Jesus performed, we'd rather keep any talk of—much more so, encounters with—demons strictly in the past. We know about schizophrenia now, and quite a few other things that make people throw themselves into fires and hide out in abandoned places. Calvin taught forthrightly that the age of miracles passed after the Scriptures came into existence.

Consider, though: humankind is rapidly acquiring expertise in understanding and manipulating the basic building blocks of life in DNA. The Scriptures tell us that angels (including fallen ones) are more intelligent and more powerful than we are and their existence predates ours. If they are as real as the Scriptures claim them to be—not cartoons, not the product of special effects—what role do Satan and his followers play?

It's to carry on a war against God.

Whatever conclusions one might come to about Winter's intriguing thoughts on science and theology and their importance for our understanding of disease, the overarching context of a war between God's rule and Satan's in the New Testament cannot be denied. Without that context, Jesus Christ's temptation in the desert, his talk of "binding the strong man [Satan]," his exorcisms, and his passion lose their meaning. Why else would Saint Paul say, "We wrestle not against flesh and blood, but against principalities, against powers, against the rulers of the darkness of this world" (Eph 6:12 KJV)?

To press the point makes us uncomfortable—that much must readily be admitted. That's not a reason, however, to dismiss Winter's thinking. If anything, it's a good reason to consider whether we truly have a biblical worldview.

For me, Winter's recasting of Genesis is helpful in enlarging our imaginations and reclaiming a truly biblical worldview. I'm not ready to give up my own understanding of the Genesis account as applying to the very beginning of creation. Part of the difficulty lies in treating what I believe to be primarily a theological document—

one that's meant to convey certain truths about God and human-kind and their relationship—and asking questions of it that it's not meant to answer. Keats' "Ode on a Grecian Urn" is about time and timelessness, not a description of ceramic techniques in the golden age of Greece. I'm not sure we can ever be positive about Genesis describing an era of creation as opposed to its origin.

Still, the connections of certain truths that Winter points out are undeniable and essential. Temptation and the resulting sin of Adam and Eve result from the work of an established opponent to God, the serpent. Our first parents' original sin by its very nature alienates them both from themselves (they suddenly realize they are naked) and from God (they hide in shame). In this context, God's judgment may be seen not so much as the imposition of God's will as a description of the consequences of their action. They have joined his opposition, and being against God strips from them the original dignity bestowed. Their sin corrupts creation, as work becomes drudgery, childbirth painful labor, and death inevitable. Although death is the "last enemy," it also keeps Adam and Eve from living a sinful existence eternally—which would have been an earthly hell—and introduces the possibility of renewed, full communion with God in the life to come.

Genesis establishes the absolute goodness of God—he makes nothing that is not good. Evil is seen as a personal force that opposes God, and creation's corruption comes about as the result of humanity's collusion with the serpent in rebellion. The creation itself begins, as Saint Paul says, to "groan," even as God promises Eve that her seed will one day crush the serpent's head, and all creation will know the glorious freedom of the children of God.

The shatteringly bright insight that Winter gained from this was that *mission* must be seen as the entire motive of the Bible—at least from the Fall and the announcement of the *proto evangelion* to Eve, and perhaps even earlier, as humankind's original purpose may have been to assist God in creation's redemption—in reclaiming the territory from Satan, whom the New Testament calls the "prince of this world" (John 12:31; 14:30; 16:11).

Christ calls us to participate in his mission to defeat all "the works of the devil," as Ralph Winter constantly repeated (1 John 3:8 NASB). We are to assist our Lord in putting all things under his feet, destroying every enemy, including the last enemy, death.

Can anyone doubt that disease participates in death as a form of life devoted to life's destruction? Disease by its nature survives not by extending God's creation but by destroying life, and when it has accomplished this mission, it dies too. Who can doubt that eradicating disease, to the extent possible, ought to be a major concern of Christ's followers?

12

GRIEF AND ITS EVIL CAUSE

Roberta Winter had been not only a loving wife but Ralph's steadfast partner—and sometimes fierce defender—in all things for nearly fifty years. From their joint study of linguistics, to their days as missionaries in Guatemala, to transforming their home into the operations center of a nascent publishing company, to the long battle to establish the U.S. Center for World Mission, Roberta and Ralph worked side by side, multiplying each other's effectiveness and recouping in love the energies they spent in their calling.

The young man who thought his calling might never allow him to marry found a wife who could hang on to the tail of this comet and enjoy the ride. Roberta was a shooting star herself.

Unlike the stereotype of the scientist with a calculator for a soul, Ralph had a deeply affectionate nature. He enjoyed family life, and his four girls—Beth, Becky, Linda, and Tricia—as they grew to womanhood, commanded his respect and admiration as well as his love. He was particularly pleased that they all chose on their own initiative to go into mission work, which speaks of what parents Roberta and Ralph were. It's common for MKs ("missionary kids") to feel that their childhoods have been unfairly sacrificed on the altar of their parents' calling.

Ralph's warmth impressed many on their first meeting. Politicians and church leaders often acquire the knack of charming people, but their solicitude is often a veneer for solicitation of one's support. Ralph drew one in as well, but he was actually interested in who you were, which bespoke real kindness and humility. As he shook one's hand, he'd smile softly, the lines around his eyes would crinkle, and his face would shine with a delighted curiosity. His enjoyment of other people was always evident.

On the other hand, he could also be straightforward in a way that took little account of social convention. His manner was an odd mix of genuine courtesy and startling candor. He conducted much of his courtship of Roberta, remember, as if it were an inter-rogation, buffeting her with questions to confirm his intuition of her fitness.

Ralph did something at least equally startling in the search for a new wife. His personal supporters will remember receiving one of Ralph's periodic newsletters in which he confessed that the single life did not suit him. He was miserable, in fact. He described himself as an "unemployed husband," and asked his network to help him find a new mate. He also enclosed a paper on which he solicited their feedback.

A long-time acquaintance, Barbara Scotchmer, responded with a critique of his article as well as advice on how he might find a new companion. The Scotchmers had been supporters of the Winters, and Barb continued after her husband died. Ralph found her reply to be the most intelligent, so he said. A myriad of phone calls, emails, and cross-country visits ensued. Barb's responses to Ralph's many questions were so thoughtful that love bloomed once more! Ralph and Barb were married in St. Louis, Missouri, on July 6, 2002, and Barb was soon swept up into the whirlwind of Ralph's activity.

During their marriage, Barb served Ralph as his editor, amanu-ensis, archivist, caregiver and, above all, loving wife. She was also his prudent counselor and, in the view of longtime associates, could persuade Ralph to do things that many others could not—like finally replacing much-needed carpeting in campus meeting rooms and installing central heating and air conditioning in their own home while restoring it following a fire just six months after they were married. I had a chance to observe the couple firsthand,

and the way Barb matched Ralph's indefatigable nature was remarkable; and her loving care for him during subsequent difficulties was nothing less than heroic.

Ralph's doctor called him in St. Louis on July 10, just after Barb and he returned from a brief honeymoon, with the diagnosis of the same form of cancer, multiple myeloma, that took Roberta. Remarkably, Ralph would live an active life for years to come and enjoyed periods of reasonably good health, for which Barb and he were grateful. From 2002 on, though, he lived in the awareness that his death might be close at hand.

He made a long entry about this on his seventy-eighth birthday, December 8, 2002, while he kept a four-hour prayer shift at the U.S. Center's prayer room.

"Today," he wrote, "I'm 78 and feel like 60. It is hard to believe that the tests last week showed the telltale signs of bone marrow cancer (myeloma) continuing steadily to increase … I feel I have learned the most important things of my life since I was 70! … Most of what I have 'learned' since I was 70 has to do with the nature of God and his Word. I have been especially fascinated by praying and meditating about the glory of God."

Ralph lamented the lack of conversation between Christians who study the book of revelation (the Bible) and scientists who study the book of creation (nature). "It is our obligation," Winter wrote, "to read, study, and worship him as we learn of the true glory of God that can be seen in both books." [56]

Winter saw the evidence of "evil intelligent design" in the creation of disease-causing pathogens as a way to renew the conversation. The lack of such a proposition, he thought, was a prime cause of many secular people's disdain for Christianity.

---

56 Winter, "How Should We Deal with the Phenomenon of Disease?" in *Frontiers*, 173.

He tried to begin such a conversation, literally, with a fellow traveler, Philip Johnson—someone he thought might immediately see the point. A leader in the intelligent design movement, Philip Johnson's book *Darwin on Trial* provoked a counteroffensive among neo-Darwinian theorists and brought the questionable validity of Darwinism to public attention in a new way in the 1990s.

Hardly shy, Ralph engaged Johnson in a dialogue at a meeting in the San Francisco Bay Area. He congratulated Johnson for proving the necessity of intelligent design in creation. Then Ralph posed this thought experiment. If Johnson saw his computer screen suddenly go blank and a dialogue box appear announcing that the computer's hard drive had been wiped clean, would he not presume his computer had been attacked by a virus? And would he not also presume that the virus had been the product of intelligent design?

Johnson said yes.

Ralph wanted to know whether it wouldn't be more proper in this case to speak not simply of "intelligent design" but "intelligent evil design."

Johnson agreed again.

Winter then asked why we couldn't say the same thing about disease-causing viruses. Could they not be the product of "intelligent evil design"?

Johnson wanted to think about that, and he did, replying to Ralph in a follow-up letter that his role was to question Darwin on scientific terms—he could not refer to God, much less Satan!

In Johnson's position he might well be wise to adopt this stance, Ralph could see. If the intelligent design community would not advance this conversation, though, who would?

Such a conversation was not only theologically important, it had broad implications for evangelization and the eradication of disease itself. To Winter's mind evangelical Christians were still caught up in a sixteenth-century understanding of the faith. The role satanic powers might have in directing microbes to create disease through DNA manipulation had never even been considered; the founders of the Reformation (and the church fathers before them) simply had no knowledge of disease-causing pathogens. "Our current theological literature, to my knowledge, does not seriously consider disease pathogens from a theological point of view—that is, are they the work of God or Satan? Much less does this literature ask the question, 'Does God mandate us to eliminate pathogens?'" [57]

One of Winter's colleagues at William Carey International University, Dr. Beth Snodderly, makes a crucial and central theological equation in her writings that helps us see Winter's point. Snodderly shows that Christ will put "every enemy under his feet, even the last enemy, death" (1 Cor. 15:25–26). Everything we know about satanic powers from Scripture connects them with corruptions of life that finally lead to death—even death as an eternal reality in hell. Everything we know of God equates his presence with healing and life. As Winter remarks, Jesus did not go around imposing sickness on people for the sake of their spiritual well-being; he healed all their diseases. Through the central equation of God with life and evil with death, Snodderly argues that we have every warrant to believe that whatever leads to death—as with disease and cataclysm—participates in evil. The absolute goodness of God is theology's first principle. God can in no way be the direct cause of disease, although, as previously discussed, all of evil, including disease, is something God permits when he grants free will.

Winter writes:

> To destroy the works of the devil is one major way in
> which our testimony of word and deed can glorify the
> true nature of our living God, our heavenly father. It is
> not an alternative to evangelism; it will make our evan-

---

gelism more credible. *It is to rectify our God's damaged reputation.* It is to avoid the implicit and embarrassing policy of almost constantly misrepresenting him in our mission work around the world. Attacking the roots of disease is part and parcel of our basic mandate to glorify God in all the earth. [58]

Who would take up the challenge of eradicating disease and showing forth God's true character? Winter had once again identified a blind spot in Christian thinking. In the same way that thousands of "people groups" were hidden, as Winter pointed out at Lausanne in 1974, so now in 2005 this task of eradicating disease as a testimony to God's glory was an area to which Christians were almost completely blind.

Certainly the care of the sick has always been a hallmark of Christian witness. In the first centuries of the church, Christians stayed in plague-infested cities to treat the sick, while pagan physicians fled. Through the ages hospital after hospital has been established around the world as part of the Christian mission. As a result, even in countries with miniscule Christian populations like Thailand, a significant percentage of the best medical care is provided in Christian hospitals. Today's pioneers of medical missions, like the late Daniel Kalnin, the founder of northern Myanmar's "barefoot doctors," find ways to bring care to poor people despite political opposition.

This witness has not extended very far, however, in regard to disease *eradication.* No doubt the prevalent atheism among numerous scientific researchers keeps many Christians from calling attention to their faith as they do basic research. Even so, the lack of a coordinated, focused effort to eliminate disease as a means of Christian witness is shocking—or should be.

---

58 Ibid., 179–80.

The need for Christians to respond to this mission is even more urgent, Winter saw, because of the way the medical community's priorities are directed by financial reward.

Science was finding that viral and other infectious agents play a role in more and more diseases. For example, ulcers were long thought to be the result of stress and spicy food before the discovery of their true cause, the bacterium *heliobacter pylori*. The role of infection in heart disease has also been well-established. Infectious agents may also be part of the story with devastating illnesses such as multiple sclerosis, mental disorders like schizophrenia, and the common killers—cancer and Alzheimer's.

At the same time, only a fraction of medical research is devoted to understanding the causal agents of disease and eradicating them. Most research concerns treating the patient's symptoms. Winter thought this was like putting on flak jackets against snipers when the real problem was to eliminate the snipers altogether.

Money tends to pave the roads that medicine travels. Billions are expended treating heart disease through bypass operations, angioplasty, stenting, and medication. What if a "simple pill" could keep infection from expanding within the arterial wall and blowing up fat deposits? That's the way most strokes and heart attacks actually happen. Even someone whose arteries narrow by as much as 90 percent can remain in reasonably good health as long as no infection-induced cardiac events occur. As yet, however, relatively little research has been conducted on the nature of arterial infection and its genesis in comparison to the huge sums spent on palliative efforts.

If there were a "simple pill" that could eliminate or mitigate arterial wall infection, it would have to be composed of an exclusive, not-so-simple formula in order to reach the market and be prescribed. Winter discovered that the cost of FDA approval for any drug runs between $400 and $800 million. This makes the drugs that are approved expensive, and guarantees that drugs that might be inexpensive to manufacture will never be submitted for approval. There would be no financial return for such an investment.

Also, medical research is by and large devoted to afflictions— such as heart disease and cancers—that are common among wealthy populations. A remedy for one of the world's most prevalent and destructive diseases, malaria, has still not been found—likely because it ceases to exist in populations with good sanitation.

The realities of financial reward direct the attention of the scientific and medical community toward *treating* disease rather than curing it.

That's why Winter so fervently believed that charitable, Christian research institutions must be founded to address eradication.

One success story underlines this point. For ages many in West Africa and elsewhere have been plagued by guinea worm. This parasite enters the body through water and then grows into a thirty-two-inch-long, host-devouring, tapewormlike creature that finally seeks to escape through the skin. It must be arduously extracted whole, wound on a stick, inch by gruesome inch, or the victim dies. Happily, guinea worm is now close to extinction as the result of the Carter Center's efforts. If President Carter, whose theological training was on par with that of many Sunday school teachers, could see the necessity of undertaking the mission of disease eradication, why couldn't others?

Christians ought to be emulating the Carter Center's efforts in research facilities by the score, Winter believed. The "return on investment" that could be anticipated would be the restoration of God's "damaged reputation," as researchers and those who supported them demonstrated God's love and glory.

∞

There's another dimension as well that might be anticipated from following through on Ralph Winter's insights into "evil intelligent design." One of the most intriguing things Behe says in his book *Darwin's Black Box* is that scientists may be blinding themselves to discoveries that could be made if they presumed the world had been designed by an intelligent agent. The *orderliness* of God's creation—because God was a reasonable God—certainly encouraged the discoveries of scientists like Boyle, Kepler, Mendel, and Newton.

What if a scientist asked himself: I wonder if pathogens are the result of intelligent, evil design? How would I, if I were a demonic agent, take an otherwise benign life-form and engineer it to cause destruction? What if cancer is not a fluke of nature but an elaborate and highly complex crime to be solved?

These questions and others like them should be asked.

The success of science in the West rested on the hypothesis of a created order. Perhaps a new age in science might begin with the hypothesis of *created disorder*.

Winter wanted scientists and theologians to think and talk about such matters. As he did in so many other instances, Ralph decided that since no one else was encouraging this conversation, he would create the forum for such a discussion. The Roberta Winter Institute (RWI) came into being, with the mission—as executive director Brian Lowther has framed it—of "demonstrating God's character through disease eradication."

The Institute intends to establish a society of "interested medical practitioners, researchers, theologians and others to investigate and discuss evidence of an intelligent evil having a destructive influence on God's good creation and the implications that notion would have on disease eradication efforts."

Lowther points out that many of the world's most difficult problems—such as poverty, illiteracy, political corruption, and spiritual darkness—have many agencies addressing them. There are *no* Christian organizations, as Winter discovered and Lowther has verified, directly concerned with disease eradication. This is a mission crying out for Christian involvement.

Winter and his colleagues have from the beginning seen the mission of the Roberta Winter Institute primarily in terms of encouraging public discussion of these matters rather than building the research facilities themselves. The main purpose of the RWI is advocacy of these ideas.

It's inspiriting to imagine, though, the Roberta Winter Institute being complemented by a research facility, the Winter Institute for Disease Eradication. At least that's my vision. Such a facility would be a witness to the true character of a loving God and a tribute to one of God's saints. Maybe it will be founded in California. Maybe South Korea or Singapore. Name almost any place on the globe and Ralph Winter is known as one of God's ambassadors there.

Those involved with the Roberta Winter Institute are praying that God will call ingenious people into the field of disease eradication as a direct Christian witness.

13

LIFE TOGETHER

Ralph Winter considered his greatest achievement the creation of an organization that as yet has barely been mentioned. Although its origins trace back to Ralph's days at Fuller Seminary and its presence made almost everything Ralph accomplished possible, it remained—and still remains—in the background. I suspect that many have my experience of getting to know the U.S. Center for World Mission, the *Perspectives* course, the books of William Carey Library, or the offerings of the William Carey International University, and take these as radiations of Ralph's brilliant mind. They were and are that, in part, but their true center has always resided in the religious order Ralph founded, the Frontier Mission Fellowship.

Immediately, the idea of a Protestant leader founding a religious order—one based loosely on the Rule of Saint Benedict—causes bewilderment among some, consternation on the part of others. Can a Protestant even do that? Aren't religious orders a Catholic thing?

History was an authority for Winter. He rediscovered his love of science through learning of the profound faith of many scientists. He tried to complete the education of undergraduates at USC while he was still a seminarian himself through teaching a class that provided historical context where it was left out due to its Christian character. In a real sense the work of William Carey International University and the courses based on the *Perspectives* curriculum were the completion of this ambition conceived in his early twenties. When he became known for his thinking about contemporary missions while at Fuller Seminary, what he taught was mainly the history of the church.

Early on, he discovered that the Reformers' characterization of monastic life as a "retreat from the world" was simply wrong. The Benedictine order brought dignity to the idea of manual labor for the first time in human history. Their monasteries were teaching and spiritual formation centers that preserved and transmitted the best of human knowledge. When Christians read the works of Augustine or Jerome—as the Reformers certainly did—they are reading the literature of *monks*. Without monastics the church would have little or nothing with which to carry on the work of Christ, including the Bible.

The monks of Iona and Lindisfarne—the *peregrini* (wanderers)—re-Christianized Europe after Rome began its long decline. Other monks, such as Saint Augustine of Canterbury and Saint Patrick, went north from Roman territory to complete the task. The great resurgence of Christianity that came about under Pope Gregory the Great was due to his formation as a Benedictine monk, when he was known as Hildebrand. Charlemagne's great assistant in the Carolingian Renaissance was Alcuin, a monk.

The monastic orders also turned the swamps of Europe into cultivated land. These foundations not only preserved traditional artisan skills but were actually centers of research and development as well, inventing many innovations in agricultural technique. The monasteries set the example of how a meritocracy—in which jobs were assigned on the basis of ability rather than rank—could outcompete a class-structured society. They were so successful in their business activities, in fact, that they soon became the bankers of their nobles and kings and helped establish a pan-European financial system that financed entrepreneurial activity.

Each monastery elected its abbot following the principle of one man/one vote—a revolutionary measure. Once elected, abbots tended to serve for life, but monasteries constantly held chapter meetings that were consultative sessions among all the community's members. The monks' democratic procedures eventually influenced the rest of society and helped break down feudalism. The first local European legislatures often met in the chapter halls of monasteries, which were often the only spaces available that were fitted for the purpose.

So Winter found the Protestant "BOBO" ("Blinking Off" after the book of Acts, and "Blinking On" again after the Reformation) view of Christian history impossible to maintain for anyone with the least interest in history or the least understanding of God's active role in history.

He believed that the religious orders were even more important to the endurance and strength of Christianity than the church's hierarchy. He found the beginnings of both the church's parish structure and its mission structure (such as religious orders) in the New Testament and their antecedents in Jewish life. The parish or local church was obviously based on the synagogues in which the Jewish diaspora—those living outside Jerusalem—regularly worshiped. Those synagogues had been planted not only by Jews seeking opportunity outside their homeland but also by Jewish missionaries. Jesus speaks to those who seek to spread Judaism "to the ends of the earth," and Paul's missionary journeys followed the example of Jewish missionaries who had spread synagogues throughout Asia Minor—some of the synagogues Paul visited in Asia Minor were probably started by these missionaries.

Winter saw that from the beginning in Christianity two types of structures existed—the local church and "second-decision" societies of missionary activity. Winter stressed that Paul and Barnabas were "sent out" from the local church in Antioch, but their activities were not governed by it. In this sense Paul, Barnabas, Timothy, Luke, and others who assisted Paul in his efforts were a self-regulating society, with Paul as the final decision maker—something like a general director or abbot—except to the degree he consulted with Peter and the other apostles in Jerusalem.

If the parish system or local church could be traced to the Jewish synagogue, the religious orders owed their genesis both to Paul and his companions and also the example of the Roman army. Winter thought first the Christian soldier, Pachomius, and then Benedict adapted characteristics of military life for the purpose of making cenobitic or communal life possible and effective, which largely replaced the eremitical (hermitlike) life that went before it.

Ralph thought that the inactivity by Protestants in missions for the first two hundred years of Protestantism's existence was due to its unfortunate elimination of the religious order structure. It was only when these spontaneously revived through William Carey and Hudson Taylor and their creation of mission agencies that the nineteenth century would become the great age of Protestant missions.

Winter understood that Protestant mission agencies were like religious orders in terms of being composed of people who had made a "second decision" to put themselves under the authority of the organization's leadership and abide by rules, regulations, and standards of conduct that went far beyond what was commonly demanded of the laity. Like the religious orders, these mission agencies were devoted to a singular purpose—the spread of the gospel in India or China—and they adopted what Winter called a "wartime lifestyle" in which the needs of the campaign were considered first and personal fulfillment a distant second.

Winter also saw that the Anabaptist tradition, in striving for small, highly dedicated communities of Christian believers, was a hybrid of the religious order and the local church. Unlike religious orders, these communities were based in the family, but the discipline accepted by adult members of Anabaptist churches made them comparable to "second-decision" organizations. We see this today among the Amish, who allow their young people to consider leaving their communities and joining the "English world" before, in most cases, accepting the peculiar obligations of adult Amish.

The early missionary societies were unfortunately known for being rigorous in the obligations of their members while, at the same time, being family-based. I have spoken to many children of missionaries who have said: "My parents made a bargain that they would attend to God's business if God would take care of their families." This meant in practice that many children of missionaries up to the 1960s and later were sent away to boarding schools— frequently, but not always, of a distinctly unpleasant kind. These children often hated God for the choice their parents had made. The Winters never made this mistake, but it's a tension that any family-based, second-decision organization must handle wisely.

Talk of religious orders made evangelical Christians nervous, as Winter well understood, and partly for this reason he invented his own nomenclature for what he was after. He adopted the traditional, if much less well-known, Catholic term "sodality" to describe a community devoted to a single purpose—what evangelicals often call a "parachurch ministry." And he used the term "modality" for the local church system, realizing that actually only made sense within his own system. The local church as a "modality" had to serve many competing interests, and so its authority structure must always tend toward the democratic, with the deliberate character democracy always brings to decision making. Sodalities, collections of individuals dedicated to a single purpose, could be governed in a far more efficient way, with most of the organization's authority resting in one person, as long as that person was ultimately accountable to a board of directors.

So Ralph and Roberta Winter brought the sodality of the Frontier Mission Fellowship (FMF) into being. The various organizations that Ralph Winter started once he left Fuller Seminary were staffed primarily by members of the Frontier Mission Fellowship. The FMF is governed by a general director, a role Ralph played until about two weeks before his death. The general director of the Frontier Mission Fellowship directs the activities of its members—in a similar fashion to an abbot directing the tasks of his monks—with due regard for their gifts and personal development. The general director has the final say in most every decision the FMF makes—as Hudson Taylor did with the China Inland Mission. The general director can be removed, however, by an internal board, to which he or she is accountable.

This made it possible for Ralph to get a great new idea, assess whether he could pull the staffing for it from members presently engaged in other activities, and then, if he did, pull the trigger. Just like that. The governing structure of the Frontier Mission Fellowship made fast decisions possible, instituting new ventures with a speed that's impossible for other types of organizations, particularly churches and schools.

That's why there are presently a baker's dozen of organizations listed at the Frontier Mission Fellowship website (www.frontier-missionfellowship.org). By virtue of its structure as a religious order, the FMF has a huge, global impact—one in which a relative handful of members address global challenges that much of the Christian world has hardly begun to recognize.

What Ralph couldn't do, though, when he wanted to implement a new initiative was post job descriptions and wait for applications to come in. The members of the Frontier Mission Fellowship raise their own support, in the tradition of Hudson Taylor's China Inland Mission (now OMF International) and other "faith missions." This has always meant that many challenges the FMF would like to address have either been understaffed (sometimes drastically) or left unaddressed.

Every organization that's started by a charismatic founder must eventually go through a transition from "a person" to "a purpose." Religious orders have always identified this purpose through reflecting on the essential gift of their founder—his charisma. The Benedictines following their founder identified humility as the source of true spirituality; humility is a gateway to seeing every activity, especially manual labor and prayer, as a means of communion with God. The Franciscans following their founder have emphasized service to the poor and utter dependence on God for all their needs.

About two weeks before Ralph Winter's death, he appointed his successor as general director of the Frontier Mission Fellowship, Dave Datema. I asked Dave what was the central organizing principle of the FMF. What impelled the members of the FMF to engage in running those thirteen organizations, and how would they decide on future new initiatives?

Dave identified Ralph Winter's essential gift—seeing previously unseen challenges to the work of Christ in the world, especially in terms of mission activities, and devising ways to address these challenges. A "frontier" for his members is anything that's been a hidden challenge to the kingdom of God reigning on earth—like those "hidden peoples" that Ralph Winter identified so stunningly in Lausanne. What unifies the efforts of the FMF is the desire to see what others miss and devise solutions. So when you look at those thirteen different organizations, as diverse as they seem, they all share this common attribute of being devoted to problems that others are not addressing.

Often, of course, the Frontier Mission Fellowship will start to address a problem and others, once aware of the problem, will start their own organizations as a response. The FMF rejoices in this and takes inspiring others in this way as one of its chief missions. It recognizes that it cannot solve the world's problems by itself. What the FMF hopes to do is make these problems visible and invent viable models for their solution that others can adapt and multiply.

The Frontier Mission Fellowship is a ministry both for visionaries—those who will come after Ralph Winter and take up his mantle as "mission engineers"—and also for people who understand management and process and can implement others' dreams.

The evangelical community is full of enthusiasm these days for "intentional communities" whose work demonstrates Christ's love to the world. As Ralph Winter showed, intentional communities have been around since Paul and Barnabas hoisted a sail. Their history includes many glorious accomplishments in Christ's name and also setbacks and problems aplenty. There's an absolutely wonderful drive that young people have to bring such communities into existence. This drive is usually best directed into energizing the work of intentional communities like the Frontier Mission Fellowship that have both vast expertise in following their callings and also the benefit of having already made their share of mistakes. Ralph always advised young people first to take a look around and see whether other Christians were already doing what they wanted to do and then to participate in what God was already doing. He did this himself. But very few could see what Ralph Winter saw, and even fewer had the will to act on what Ralph saw.

The amazing thing about the Frontier Mission Fellowship is that it's *not* devoted to the "same old thing." It's explicitly devoted to finding new frontiers of the kingdom; to seeing God's "will be done on earth as it is in heaven"; to exploring the terrain for the first time and figuring out how to establish encampments of God's kingdom. For an earthly institution, the opportunities are about as limitless as God himself.

14

THE ROLE OF A LIFETIME
BECOMES A LEGACY

Ralph Winter said that in the last years of his life, from the time he turned seventy years of age, his greatest joy was what he had learned about the Bible. This was a remarkable statement from a man who had studied the Scriptures diligently from his youth and had gone to great lengths to do so.

He began as a teenager through Christian Endeavor and his time in the Navigators, memorizing hundreds of Bible verses. He spent time at Westmont College and Princeton Seminary specifically to learn about inductive Bible study, and traveled to Prairie Bible Institute to become familiar with its question-and-answer method. He learned much at Fuller Seminary and a second stint at Princeton, and earned advanced degrees at Columbia and Cornell in order to translate what he knew into other languages and cultures. He taught and preached on Scripture throughout his life, from the mountains of Guatemala to every corner of the globe. One wouldn't think that he'd have to wait until old age for the Bible to divulge its richest treasures.

What he meant, I think, concerned both the insights he had gained and also the person he had become. First through "kingdom theology," which emphasizes how God seeks to establish his reign in a world otherwise ruled by evil, and second through his inquiry into the nature of evil, which led to his reinterpretation of Genesis, he came to see missions as the fundamental context of the Bible and human history. Humankind was created and exists in order to assist God in his reclamation of creation. That's the spine of the historical story; everything else derives its meaning from this central theme.

Ralph certainly found the meaning of his life within this context as well, in a most unusual way, however. His early life was dominated by far more seeking than finding. He was frustrated, I believe, by his enormous appetite for and pleasure in the work of God and by God's silence about exactly how he wanted Ralph to use his talents in God's service. He finally made the decision to be ordained not on the basis of a "call," as most understand this, meaning a watershed encounter with God marked by high emotion, but simply by reasoning out that people would be more inclined to listen to his ideas if he had the credential. There's a clichéd way to think of this, and that is that Ralph, as someone with a scientific disposition, a "Mr. Wizard," simply wasn't the type of emotional person who has such experiences—his character was too dominated by reason. That's not who Ralph Winter was, though. He was a kind, loving husband and father, a warm friend, and a deeply passionate man. He came to know God intimately, I believe, as few others do.

In "The Ascent of Mount Carmel," Saint John of the Cross writes:

> *To come to the knowledge you have not*
> *You must go by a way in which you know not.*
>
> *To come to be what you are not*
> *You must go by a way in which you are not.*

I love these lines, however difficult they may be, because they speak to how a sometimes-hidden God can use his concealment to accomplish his purpose. God kept what he ultimately had in store for Ralph hidden for years and years. Ralph had to follow the trail of assignments God gave him—like an orienteer using

a map and compass to make his way through unknown terrain—
before Ralph could describe the landscape and recognize his place
within it. Only after completing a long, preparatory itinerary could
he articulate his unique role, first explaining it to his own satisfac-
tion and then to others' comprehension.

Ralph Winter was a genius who put his gifts to work as a
problem solver for God. His colleagues, family, and friends may
be shy about such a description, but think of the nature of the
gifts of someone who can graduate from Caltech in two and a half
years, earn a doctorate in linguistics from Cornell with little prior
preparation, teach himself to play piano chords by checking a
book out of the library, and master accounting late at night after
a full day as a missionary. That list does not even address the
thousand and one ideas and organizations he launched in the
field of missions. He was a genius who was compelled in ways
that only genius knows.

Ralph Winter was also a mystery to people, to the point of
provoking hostile reactions; but no more a mystery to others,
I think, than he was to himself, at least as a young man. Roberta
would "defend him" much later by saying he was not a great
speaker or writer but a visionary who saw problems others could
not and who thought of solutions no one else would even consider.

In his youth there was no category for such a person—no slot
for Ralph's idiosyncratic peg as missions engineer and global
mobilizer. He had to grow into his identity, see its usefulness,
and then embrace it despite what others might think. That took
a long period of acting on what he did know without seeing the
big picture. He couldn't know the way ("to come to the knowledge
you have not," as the poet puts it) if he was to come to understand
a role in life—his role—that had yet to be invented. He could only
come to be what God made him by trailblazing. This took hacking
his way forward while feeling lost at times. It also took humility—
his fascination with problems and solutions to the exclusion of any

interest in power and fame. That's a lot of going "by a way in which you are not," as the poet describes the type of self-forgetfulness that characterized Ralph Winter.

In fact, I don't think Ralph understood the fullness of his vocation until he ventured out into the Frontier Mission Fellowship and the U.S. Center for World Mission. Earlier on, he began to describe himself as a missions engineer, but only his religious community and its projects allowed him to abandon himself to this role. He was not quite fifty years old when he gave his famous speech in Lausanne in 1974. Two years later the U.S. Center began operations. That's a long, long time for a man to realize the fullness of his calling.

Even then Ralph began this new endeavor in fear and trembling, even if he understood that it perfectly suited his talents. Many of his former colleagues believed he would only make a fool of himself and shed a negative light on them in doing so. God blessed him in it, I believe, because of Ralph's faithfulness and stewardship of the gifts God gave him, and also as a means of blessing to future generations of people with similar gifts through the Frontier Mission Fellowship. So often, God sets a pattern with one faithful man and then uses that man's faithfulness for God's own larger and ever-expanding purposes.

In his later years Ralph gained something even deeper than his profound understanding of the Bible's context and how his own life fit into this context. In the famous journalist and TV commentator Malcolm Muggeridge's later years, he was fond of saying that as he drifted off to sleep at night, reciting the Lord's Prayer, he was more convinced of God's reality than he was his own. Evangelical Christians commonly speak of a personal relationship with God through Jesus Christ. In my experience, it's rare to meet an evangelical Christian—or any Christian, for that matter—whose belief in "my God" is as palpable as was Ralph's. He took *offense* at people blaming disease and other evils on God, as one would take offense at others casting aspersions on a family member. Ralph showed his jealousy for God's reputation freely to the world. What he could not show, but hinted at through his later writings, was his deep communion with God through the Scriptures. He knew God. He knew God because he visited with God daily through prayer and reading of the Scriptures, often for hours at a time. He arrived at a faith many yearn for, others pretend to have, but few actually possess. Jesus called his disciples not merely servants but friends—to be the Lord's friend was Ralph's highest aspiration.

Even before Ralph married Barb in 2002, he was diagnosed with Lyme disease. This deprived him of his usual dynamic energy more often even than his bone marrow cancer, which went into remission for long periods of time. His medical condition became even more complicated when in early 2009 he was diagnosed with another form of cancer—lymphoma. Even so, when I came to know him personally during the last two years of his life, he worked and traveled virtually nonstop. His sense of time running out made him more committed than ever. I remember visiting with him in his hospital room at eight and nine o'clock in the evening (at his request), and observing as he sat up and dictated memos and reviewed organizational matters with his wife, Barb, and associates like Beth Snodderly, then provost of William Carey International University. I was beat. He had a couple of hours left before sleep that he intended to use!

In May of 2009 the doctors could do nothing more for Ralph and he came home. On the twentieth, with three of his daughters— Becky, Linda, and Beth—around his bed, along with his wife, Barb, singing hymns as they kept watch, Ralph died at age eighty-four.

Few have fought the good fight as Ralph Winter did or left such a remarkable legacy of people and organizations that continue to play the role this social engineer invented for the glory, not of himself, but of God and the spread of his kingdom. As Ralph frequently said, "I am willing to fail. Risks are not to be evaluated in terms of the probability of success, but in terms of the value of the goal."

BIBLIOGRAPHY

Ellisen, S. A. "Everyone's Question: What Is God Trying to Do?" In *Perspectives on the World Christian Movement: A Reader*, 4th ed., edited by R. D. Winter and S. C. Hawthorne, 17–20. Pasadena: William Carey Library, 2009.

McGavran, D. A., and G. G. Hunter. *Church Growth: Strategies that Work*. Nashville: Abingdon, 1980.

McPhee, A. G. *Pickett's Fire: The Life, Contribution, Thought, and Legacy of J. Waskom Pickett, Methodist Missionary to India*. Wilmore, KY: Asbury Theological Seminary, 2000.

Parsons, G. H. "Ralph D. Winter's Life and Legacy: Missiology, Vision and Strategy." Unpublished PhD dissertation, University of Wales, 2009 draft.

———. "Ralph D. Winter: Life and Core Missiology." PhD diss., University of Wales, 2012.

Shenk, W. R., and G. R. Hunsberger. *American Society of Missiology: The First Quarter Century*. Decatur, GA, 1998.

Snodderly, B. *The Goal of International Development: God's Will on Earth, as It Is in Heaven*. Pasadena: William Carey International University Press, 2009.

———. "A Socio-Rhetorical Investigation of the Johannine Understanding of 'the Works of the Devil' in 1 John 3:8." PhD diss., University of South Africa, 2009.

Winter, R. D. "A Blindspot in Western Christianity?" In *Frontiers in Mission*, 200–202. Pasadena: William Carey International University Press, 2008.

———. *Frontiers in Mission: Discovering and Surmounting Barriers to the Missio Dei*. Pasadena: William Carey International University Press, 2008.

————. "A Growing Awareness about Disease." In *Frontiers in Mission*, 175–76. Pasadena: William Carey International University Press, 2008.

————. "The Highest Priority: Cross-Cultural Evangelism." In *Let the Earth Hear His Voice: International Congress on World Evangelization, Lausanne, Switzerland,* edited by J. D. Douglas, 213–25. Minneapolis: World Wide, 1975.

————. "How Should We Deal with the Phenomenon of Disease?" In *Frontiers in Mission*, 173–74. Pasadena: William Carey International University Press, 2008.

————. "Impacts, Eruptions and Major Mass Extinctions." In *Frontiers in Mission*, 223–24. Pasadena: William Carey International University Press, 2008.

————. "The Kingdom Strikes Back." In *Frontiers in Mission*, 93–103. Pasadena: William Carey International University Press, 2008.

————. "Making Sense to Today's Scientists." In *Frontiers in Mission*, 240–43. Pasadena: William Carey International University Press, 2008.

————. "Planetary Events and the Mission of the Church." In *Frontiers in Mission*, 290–91. Pasadena: William Carey International University Press, 2008.

————. "Theologizing the Microbiological World." In *Frontiers in Mission*, 203–5. Pasadena: William Carey International University Press, 2008.

————. "The Unfinished Epic." In *Frontiers in Mission*, 317–26. Pasadena: William Carey International University Press, 2008.

————. "Where Darwin Scores Higher than Intelligent Design." In *Frontiers in Mission*, 191–94. Pasadena: William Carey International University Press, 2008.

Winter, R. H. "Winter Initiatives." Unpublished document, Pasadena, 2000.

roberta winter institute

Exploring God's Will in Relation to Disease and Evil

It is my genuine hope that you enjoyed this narrative approach to Ralph Winter's life and thought and that your curiosity was piqued about the ongoing work of the Roberta Winter Institute (RWI).

You see, though its founder passed away in 2009, the Roberta Winter Institute continues on with fresh conviction and vision. That vision is to inspire faith-based initiatives to address the roots of disease. Toward this vision, we publish resources, sponsor gatherings and pursue relationships that will help a large, general audience connect with our mission and make it their own.

One of our key outlets is the RWI website and blog. There you can explore with us as we examine questions about God's will for humanity regarding the troubling presence of disease and evil in the world.

I urge you to visit our website often (or subscribe to our news feed!) and help us make sense of things by contributing your own theories, filling in the gaps in our knowledge base, and posing new questions we haven't thought of yet. Or, contact us directly at *info@robertawinterinstitute.org* and we will gladly begin a dialogue with you.

Brian Lowther, Director
Roberta Winter Institute

Pasadena, California